NEWBURY
A Photographic Record 1850-1935
Revised Edition

NEWBURY
A Photographic Record 1850-1935
Revised Edition

SUE HOPSON

GOLDWELL PUBLISHING

NEWBURY, BERKSHIRE

This book is dedicated to my late father-in-law
Geoffrey Paul Hopson

The photograph on the front cover
shows Miss A.G. Mathews (later Mrs A. Gould)
at the back of Basing & Mathews — harness makers
and saddlers Mansion House Street. c1905. J. Gould

First Published 1983
by Countryside Books of Newbury

Goldwell Publishing
c/o Binder Hamlyn
Sundial House, Cheap Street
Newbury, Berkshire RG14 5DH

ISBN 0 9513132 1 5

The photograph overleaf shows
Northbrook Street as it was around 1870.
Originally loaned by Mrs. K. Fishers
and donated by her to Newbury District Museum.

Original design by Mon Mohan

Produced by MRM Associates Ltd., Reading

Acknowledgements

The publishers, Suzanne and Nicholas Battle; this book was their initial idea, I hope it is all they envisaged it to be. Their professional approach was appreciated. My thanks also to Martin Marwood, Countryside Books Production Manager, for his patience; and to Mon Mohan for his skilful and evocative design of the book.

The contributors of the various photographs, who so generously delved in their attics and stripped their walls; to them, and to those who kindly gave of their time to talk of old Newbury and its inhabitants, my thanks. Without them this book would not have been possible.

Newbury District Museum Curator, Tony Higgott, for his moral support and erudite observations regarding the text, enabling the content to be more complete; also his staff, Joan Bates, Babs Meads and Virginia Field for their unfailing stoic good humour over the past few months.

The Managing Director and Editor of the *Newbury Weekly News* for giving free access to their invaluable back numbers, files, and Library.

Helen Purvis FLA for allowing herself to be coerced into accompanying me on the only sunny Sunday in May to identify the present locations of depicted buildings and for other valuable local information.

To the following for specialised information on such diverse subjects as canals, cars, railways, photography, and life in general — Dr. Sadie Ward (Museum of English Rural Life), Dave Cannings, Brian Coe (Curator, Kodak Museum), Alastair Duff, Nick Georgano, Bob Gibbs, John Gould, Dave Stubbs, and George Suggett.

All reproduction photographic work from the original photographs (except Berkshire Archeological Society & Museum of English Rural Life) has been carried out by E.C. Paine Limited of Newbury — my grateful thanks to Pete Bloodworth for his personal involvement and expertise.

Joy Clarke and Tig Robinson, my sisters-in-law for being able to make full use of the photographic material belonging to the Hopson family.

Lastly, but by no means least, my husband for his encouragement and extreme good humour throughout all the vicissitudes of compiling this book.

Preface

Although I was born in Newbury, my recollection of the town in my early years remains blurred, except for a couple of indelible memories, both of which are depicted within these pages.

It was only some twelve years ago, when my late father-in-law was reminiscing about the town and its characters in his younger days, that I began to realise the vitality of Newbury in a personal sense. Alas, almost too late, much of the soul of the town seemed to have disappeared. It may also appear to the reader that over the past decade Newbury has lost its central core and direction — time alone will be the judge?

However, we are fortunate to have our own Museum with its unique architecture, containing many diverse items depicting the life and history of Newbury and its district, whose Curator and staff are fully conscious of the urgent need to preserve for posterity any artefact, be it Stone Age axehead, photograph, document, or Edwardian costume. It would be appropriate to add here a personal note of thanks to those who have recently donated the original photographs used in this book to our Museum — it is indeed a generous gesture to share with others our treasured possessions.

I hope that these photographs may evoke nostalgic memories for some, and enable those who have moved into the town and its neighbourhood in the last twenty years, to visualise Newbury and its inhabitants in days gone by.

Only photographic material has been used in this work (except in one instance), solely because the camera lens does not lie; paintings and etchings are an interpretation of the artist's eye and imagination.

The owner is indicated beneath each photograph, except for those in the possession of the Hopson family. A list of the commercial photographers (where known) is given on the closing page.

Where applicable, squared brackets have been used during and at the end of each caption giving the present-day business or area depicted in the photograph.

S.H. — July 1983

Preface to the Revised Edition

This book has been out of print for over 6 years; local book shops have asked on numerous occasions for a reprint, perhaps 12 years after its original publication in 1983 is an appropriate time.

The text is basically as originally produced in 1983, but with a few text corrections and minor revisions in the light of new research. My thanks to those who contacted me with new or corrected information over the past 12 years, and to the generous owners of some of the photographs who subsequently donated the original photograph to Newbury District Museum.

Some of the 1983 areas/businesses within squared brackets have, perforce, changed in the past 12 years and are not necessarily the 1995 businesses at that particular location, i.e. Plate No. 9 is given as ''[Tesco]'' in 1983, in 1995 is now Mothercare.

My thanks to Martin Marwood of MRM for undertaking this reprint, and to Nicholas & Suzanne Battle of Countryside Books, the original publishers, for permission to utilise the 1983 artwork.

S.H. – September 1995

The ANCHOR.
SOUTH BERKS BREWERY Co
TO THE SALVATION ARMY HALL
95

1

1 June 22 1911 Northbrook Street Mrs. J. Camp
King George V's Coronation was the last occasion on which the town decorated itself in the time-honoured way with green garlands; even so, some folk were put out that the usual free dinner for the public was not provided.
This marvellous photograph shows the tremendous local enthusiasm for "events", even though the day was marred by showers, just about everyone turned out in their Sunday best to watch the parade go by. This particular photo, one of three, depicts the tableau by the Newbury Guildhall Club of the Last Eleven at Maiwand (Afghanistan) — a heroic stand by the remnants of the Berks. Regiment on July 27 1880. It is followed by the League of Pity car "Angel of Mercy". The steam engine behind pulls an entry by the Greenham Rifle Club of the "Development of English Weapons", and behind them although not visible here, was the Mayoral procession.

2 April 25 1908 St. Nicolas Church from Northcroft Lane
A freak snowstorm started Friday night, by Saturday morning the snow was 18" deep in places. Bakers were unable to deliver, country carriers were delayed or marooned for hours in drifts in the outlying areas. A crazy swallow was noted flying around Newbury Bridge during the Saturday morning at the height of the storm! The shops closed on Saturday at 6pm instead of the usual 10pm. A bye-law had decreed after an 1881 snowstorm that house-holders had to clear the snow from their frontages, those that did not were visited on Sunday morning by the Police and instructed to so do. By Sunday evening the snow was beginning to melt.
Postcards have been seen of the 1908 snowstorm from Odiham up to beyond Oxford.

2

3

3 February 1883 Northcroft Lane Newbury District Museum

Previous floods had been experienced in 1814 and 1871. In the 1883 flood it poured all Saturday and Sunday. Northcroft Lane is depicted here. The Drummers Beerhouse [Sutton & Griffin] is on the left. Near the Temperance Hall [Arts Workshop] a man with his trousers rolled up gives his son a piggy-back. The cattle in Northcroft had to be rescued and Waterloo Place was under several feet of water. On Monday the Fire Brigade "disported themselves in canoes in West-Street" and by Tuesday Northbrook Street had experienced such severe flooding a trench was dug across the street to Alton Place [Park Street] to allow the water to drain into the Marsh [Victoria Park]. The River Lambourn also overflowed at Shaw, and the view westwards from the Parish Church tower was one large lake.

4

5

4 1908 Newbury United Temperance Band
The Temperance movement was founded in the Victorian era to combat the evils of alcohol. In the 1800's, for every 100 of the population of Newbury there was a "house" selling some form of alcohol. The local Temperance Hall, opened in 1875 [Arts Workshop] was completely undenominational, every local Minister whatever his creed supporting their aims.
Mr. J.S. Liddle (1853-1921) came to Newbury in 1884 as organist at the Parish Church, amongst many of his activities he was instrumental in founding the Newbury Choral Society and the Temperance Band, and is seen here seated to the right of the uniformed band player in the middle, Joseph H. Hopson on the left.

5 c1880? Mayor of Northcroft? Mrs. A. Wyatt
It is thought that this gentleman, looking rather uncomfortable in his ill-fitting costume, is a rare photograph of the Mayor of Northcutt (Northcroft). Very little is known about this perhaps annually elected dignatory, except that he was nominally overseer of Northcroft and had the powers to allow or prevent folk free grazing of their livestock on the "lammas lands" at Northcroft. Photographed by Harbut of 12 Northcroft Lane, against a typical Victorian photographer's painted backcloth of rustic scene with steps.
It is possible the person portrayed is John Hall, a bricklayer living in Northcroft Lane, whose forbears and descendants lived in the Northcroft area for a century, carrying on the same trade until the 1920's.

6

HILTONS
GARAGE
DRAPERY BAZAAR
Northbrook Street, Newbury. Nº 4453.

7

8

6 1932 Northcroft Football Club B. Bowness
Photographed at the Town Football Ground, winners of the Reading Town Junior Cup, Newbury Hospital Cup and Champions of Newbury Junior League.
Top row left-right
Reg Bosley — Hon. Treasurer. Bill Champ — Hon. Secretary. Bob Davis, Albie Seymour, Ted Jones
Middle row — Ted Lawrence — Chairman. Harry Pearson. Billy Lock — Captain. Wally Bowness. Wally Parsons. Arthur Prisnall — Vice Chairman. Perce Anken — trainer
Front row — Warner Taylor. Wally Clinch. Reg Fletcher. George Rosier. Gordy Bowden. Names supplied by Gordy Bowden.

7 c1915 Northbrook Street
The end of an era, the horse and trap gives way to an open tourer approaching Newbury Bridge. York House, once the home of architect John Money, brother of Walter, Newbury's historian, dominated the vista down Northbrook Street until 1929 when the present hexagonal clock tower was erected. It has been said the Jubilee clock face (see Plate 30) is incorporated into the present clock, however the previous clock had Roman numerals, the present face has a triangular digit marking each hour.

8 c1905 84 Northbrook Street
One of Newbury's best known commercial photographers. C. Hawker took over E.T. Brooks' business early in the 1800's, along with many of his plates and photographs from c1865; some are probably depicted in this book — where are the remainder? Hawker's son Charles Adrian went off cattle ranching to the Argentine in 1903 but had apparently returned by the time this photograph was taken. [Rumbelows]

9

9 c1905 79 Northbrook Street J. Stradling
A cycle repair shop was started by (Alderman) James Stradling, Alfred's son (see plate 10) in 1877 at the rear of 77 Northbrook Street [Silvers], moving to No. 79 by 1893. James invented and made his own "Strad" bicycle and by the turn of the century had joined with Edward Plenty and set up as agents for the German Benz cars. During World War I the company made shell cases for trench mortars. After his retirement James's four sons continued in the business. [Tesco]

10 c1895 78 Northbrook Street
Founded in 1866 by Alfred Stradling, a clock maker (see plate 9). Although his son James was apprenticed into the trade, one of his other sons, Charles seen in the doorway, followed his father in the business, continuing until the first World War when the premises were sold to F.W. Gibson, jewellers from the Arcade. A three-storied building with an attractive decorative facade, a cross-barred gas street lamp on the corner. [Harry Fenton]

10

11

12

11 c1876 64 Northbrook Street & 86-91 West Street Camp Hopson & Co. Ltd.
The original Georgian building of Hopson & Sons, founded by (Alderman) Joseph Hopson at No.65 as a photographer, decorator and paperhanger in 1854. By 1860 he was trading solely in furniture and upholstery. A fine view down West Street, most of which has now been demolished. Shopping was a hazard in those days, the traders displaying their wares on the pavements and there was also a large amount of scaffolding to negotiate at the lower end of West Street. The street crossing places were cobbled as shown here.

12 June 1897 64/5 Northbrook Street Camp Hopson & Co. Ltd.
The elegant Georgian building has been entirely demolished, an unusual over-elaborate "Swiss-Mauresque" three-storied building was erected on the site in 1877. The distinctive green roof tiles were originally purchased by Mr. Winterbottom (of Tile Barn, Woolton Hill) at the 1855 Paris Exhibition and perhaps purchased by Joseph Hopson in 1869 at the Executor's 10-day sale. The building was demolished in 1968 although the terracotta religious panel has been incorporated into the new building. [Halfords]

13

14

14 c1906 Wesleyan Methodist Church choir
Mrs. B Webb

John Wesley, founder of the Wesleyan movement, often preached in Newbury during the 1700's. Their church was built on its present site in 1839, the Wesley Hall alongside in 1887, the church also ran a non-denominational day school. An appeal for funds to renovate the church has just been launched since its reprieve from demolition.

Some of the choir are known, back row left to right

__, Rupert Dolton, __, Steptoe, chapel keeper and organ blower, H.S. Dolton, Henry Michell, choirmaster and blacksmith, S.J.L. Vincent, organist and Borough Surveyor, none of the other members standing are known. Seated, __, __, __, Margaret Dolton, __, __, Edith Dolton, Florence Burrows, Nancy Burrows, Mrs. Mitchell, __ Frost, Sarah Ann Fiddler, the two boys are Charley Noakes and Charley Mitchell.

its present site in 1839, the Wesley Hall alongside in 1887, the church also ran a non-denominational day school. An appeal for funds to renovate the church has just been launched since its reprieve from demolition.

Some of the choir are known, back row left to right

__, Rupert Dolton, __, Steptoe, chapel keeper and organ blower, H.S. Dolton, Henry Michell, choirmaster and blacksmith, J.L. Vincent, organist and Borough Surveyor, none of the other members standing are known. Seated, __, __, __, Margaret Dolton, __, __, Edith Dolton, Florence Burrows, Nancy Burrows, Mrs. Mitchell, __ Frost, Sarah Ann Fiddler, the two boys are Charley Noakes and Charley Mitchell.

15

15 c1925 Elliotts Moulding & Joinery Ltd. Mill
Mrs. D.L. Buckingham

Elliotts Moulding & Joinery Co. was created by the creditors out of the "ashes" of Samuel Elliott's Steam joinery works. In 1902 he and his sons declined to renew their contracts of employment and moved to Caversham. In 1904 Edward de Vere Buckingham from Gainsborough, was appointed General Manager. In 1908 he invented a folding revolving door, but unfortunately allowed the patent to lapse! During World War I the company manufactured over 200,000 ammunition cases on machinery designed by Edward using unskilled labour. By 1926, owing to Edward's ill-health, his sons Horace & Cecil were virtually running the company. In World War II Elliotts were one of only 26 British companies licensed to manufacture whole aircraft and made (amongst other machines) 750 Airspeed "Oxford" advanced trainers, also "Horsa" gliders for the Normandy D-Day landings. After the war the Company was refused a licence to revert to their pre-war trade; it was only through the persistent intervention in Parliament of Anthony (later Lord) Hurd, our MP, that Elliotts returned to furniture manufacture in 1948. Meanwhile the company were building pre-fabricated houses (some were occupied in Westfields for 30 years), "Olympia" gliders and the "Newbury EON" a light aeroplane, to their own designs. Cecil died in 1953 and my father, Horace, in 1965. The Company ceased to trade on the Albert Works site in 1974.

[Bayer (UK) Headquarters]

16 c1860 57 Northbrook Street M. Tanner

An interesting early photograph of the Monument Inn selling Blatch's Ale from their Theale Brewery — of interest as it is the only record known of No.58 before it was demolished, the premises owned by Sam Biddis, plumber, decorator and sign writer. The Wesleyan church cupola can be seen over the Inn roof and next door is Miss Godding, sister of J.H. Godding (see plate 23) selling stationery, books and sheet music. As photography was still in its infancy the photograph can only be roughly dated; in Newbury District Museum there is a companion print of the Congregational Church in the same vignette format. A further point of interest, the painted wooden sign between the gables of the Inn is purported to be a local memorial to those who died in the Great Plague of 1665, and is said to now be buried behind the plaster inside the Inn.

17 c1912 54-64 Northbrook Street
Hopson & Sons turret at the entrance to West Street gives a start to an interesting view of the lower west side of Northbrook Street. J.J. Davies at No.63 is a listed part 17th century building; at time of writing McDonalds hamburger chain wish to take over part of the proposed new building — demolition approval is awaited from the Department of the Environment. Next door, the Newbury Building Society office, the Liberal Club, and the three-storied Technical Institute, from 1905-10 Newbury Girls School [Brook House]. The white painted Newbury Picture Palace opened its doors a month after Jimmy Tufnail's cinema at 64 Cheap Street; it was more expensive than his, the seats were 3d, 6d and 1/- in the balcony, seats bookable at W.H. Smith's on the bridge. The entrance to Elliotts Moulding & Joinery works is alongside the neat iron rails and pillars of the Wesleyan church. Next door is the 17th century Monument Inn — amazing how many public houses were next to churches and schools, the Parish Church rooms were next door to the Two Brewers Inn and surrounded by the South Berks Brewery.

16

Hamblin the tailor and Deacons grocers are next to William Gamble newsagent, publisher of this card, and advertisement office for the Marlborough Times. The building right in the corner projecting into the roadway was the George & Dragon Inn, the last building before Speenhamland, the North Brook running from Goldwell Park and under Northbrook Street to emerge in Victoria Park, being the old Parish Boundary.

17

18

18 c1885 Speenhamland Lamp G. Collier
In 1828 the obelisk was erected by subscription from the Speenhamland inhabitants, made of solid stone from a Bath quarry owned by Frederick Page of Goldwell House. It is photographed prior to the subsequent removal of the obelisk to the Speen Lane/(Old) Bath Road junction in 1899.
An earlier lithograph shows the obelisk enclosed by an iron fence with small stone pillars at each corner, and gives an indication that there was a pump behind the obelisk. In the photograph the pump is out of use, and water is obtained by the use of the water key and piece of hose at the boy's feet. Piped water was available in 1878.
It does seem whimsical that the more traffic increased the larger the edifices became, the present clock obsuring a substantial portion of the northern aspect of the Broadway.

19 c1907 Oxford Street
Edward Martin's motor works with a de Dion car in the yard entrance; the next building up the road has been demolished. The Chequers Hotel is just visible on the right, and at the junction of the Bath & Oxford roads the white-painted Wells Bakery can be seen previously a Toll House, demolished in 1950. "Teddy" Martin, for many years Captain of the Volunteer Fire Brigade, had amalgamated with Percy Chillingworth by 1910.

20 c1930 14/18 Oxford Street
Mrs. G. Lewendon
The family grocery business was founded in Speen by 1876 and moved to Oxford Street in the early 1880's, the company gradually expanding into other spheres of commerce around the turn of the century. The famous Speenhamland Theatre was behind in Gilder's Square. The days of leisurely cruises can be recalled by the notice on No.14 and the coloured posters of the luxurious cruise liners. Lewendons were also agents for those who wished to emigrate to the Dominions.
Being born just up the road, my earliest memories are the smell of newly baked bread at Wells Bakery and the inexhaustable kindly patience of the late Mr. Lewendon, shown here in his doorway, with an inquisitive seven year old exploring through his "Aladdin's Cave" of every kind of article imaginable.
[Oxford House office block]

Oxford Street, Newbury
R. MARTIN & SON.
MOTOR WORKS
GARAGE
PETROL

19

18. Antique & Modern Furniture
Cabinet Maker
Upholsterer
LEWENDON
Picture Frame
Manufacturer
STEAMSHIP BOOKING AGENT
Passages to All Parts of the World

20

21

22

21 c1890 Oxford Street Newbury Weekly News

A couple of nurserymen, stopped in the middle of the road, are delivering what appears to be a potted palm to Albion House. One of the men is supported by a crutch. A lad is leaning on Pound's the stonemason's wall, an old trough is propped up against the wall of a small shop. From this point in the photograph, going left to right, we have: an entrance to Gilder's Square before Mr. Lewendon's shop and Jacksons the tailor; the other entrance to Gilder's Square; Steptoe, his barber's pole over the window; the Bacon Arms Hotel advertising sleeping quarters for members of the Cycle Touring Club; next door is Richard Ravenor, plumber — he painted the Jubilee clock in the Broadway. The Chequers Hotel, with its upturned gas lamp, follows, and then a charming bow-fronted house [entrance to Chequers yard], James Adnams' house and his Brewery entrance beyond, also known as Speenhamland Brewery, established in 1802. Behind the present La Riveria restaurant some of the old Brewery buildings still remain, best seen from Pelican Lane. A fascinating photograph showing the mixture of roof levels, chimney pots and windows.

22 1906 Police Tug-of-War team, Newbury Division

The Berkshire Constabulary was founded by Act of Parliament in 1856. The 1904 County Police station in Pelican Lane is still standing [Berks. C.C. Youth Action Centre], the Division moving to new premises adjacent to the Ring Road in 1965. Inspector Indge of the Newbury Division compiled the 100 year history of the Berkshire Constabulary for their centenary in 1956. By 1894 bicycles were in general use, in the 1970's "Panda" cars were the accepted form of conveyance; however the 1980's policy is a return to bicycles and feet

in order to re-establish contact with the public.
Superintendent John Gamble (1905-19) is shown seated second from the left in regulation braided jacket, with his Tug-of-War team, who won the Inter-divisional cup in 1903, 1905 & 1906.

23

23 c1865 Newbury & Speenhamland Bowling Green Club Newbury Bowling Club
By 1571 bowls were being played at the rear of the Pelican Inn. The Club, the second oldest in the country, was founded in 1598. In 1845, the green was moved to the north side of Pelican Lane. Much horror was caused in 1910 when it was suggested the green should be levelled and corner to corner bowling should cease, as stated by the rules of the English Bowling Association. A happy compromise was reached — the green was levelled and corner to corner bowling was allowed on certain evenings. During 1934 the Club moved to Victoria Park, the amenities being built using unemployed labour.
This rare old photograph is fortunately named, so it is possible to give some details of the depicted players. Left to right — "Boy" in a traditional smock, who probably kept the green swept and cut. W. Clarke a draper of 6 Northbrook Street. — Swan who was Secretary 1856-71. Thomas Gurney, President 1857-84, manager of London & Counties Bank. T. Chapman? Edmund Godding who had a piano warehouse at 55 Northbrook Street. R. Ransom? James P. Jackson, President 1884-93, ironmonger in the Market Place. John Moss ran a school in Speenhamland. James H. Godding, a Professor of Music living in the London Road, the original owner of the photograph. Edwin and Sydney Forster, wine & spirit merchants of Speenhamland and 15 Northbrook Street. George Drew a veterinary surgeon of Speenhamland.
[British Legion Hall]

24

24 c1930 St. Joseph's Infant School
St. Joseph's Church
St. Joseph's was founded in 1853 at 105 London Road, the present Presbytery, by the priests of St. Mary's College, Woolhampton. Two years later the first resident priest Father Hodgson started a small school; concurrently the Misses Barratt rented a cottage in the "Rose & Thistle" yard [Pembroke Road] to establish a private Catholic school. In 1864 a small Church was built adjoining the Presbytery, the following year Canon Riley built a small school from his own funds. Work on the new Church, built by Hoskings & Pond, began in 1926 and opened in 1928, under the guidance of Canon Francis Green, seen here on the right with Father Nagel on the left with their young pupils photographed in the playground behind the Presbytery.

25

25 c1908 The Dower House
An outstanding Queen Anne house, built in 1749, stated to have been one of the finest in the country; at one time the Kings Arms Inn. It was tragically demolished in 1956. All but the Georgian west wing (not shown here) is said to have been built in 1759 by James Clarke who built Newbury Bridge. By 1794 it was owned by the brothers John and Thomas Padbury, coach and harness makers, remaining in their family until the 1880's when the Penford family lived there, the house then being named The Shrubbery (not to be confused with a house of the same name in Oxford

26

Road). By 1910 Frank Irving had purchased the property and was selling antique furniture at The Dower House. After World War I Reginald Clifford took over the property and continued in the business of selling fine antiques, his son John following him. [Wheelers car park]

26 c1906 London Road looking west
On the south side near the Jubilee Clock, consisting of mostly mid-Georgian buildings, can be seen the barber's pole of Featherstones and a first-floor bay window at Westbourne House. Watts the boot repairer and Mrs. Legg's "Registry office for Servants" have hanging signs just before the barely discernible entrance to St. Stephen's Place. On the north side is the re-built Cross Keys Inn with "good stabling and loose boxes", still there to-day. Gregory's coal & corn merchant is next door, Mrs. Shuff, and then Mrs. Bowley the dressmaker who lived next to the Star Inn [Cromwells Wine Bar] owned by the South Berks Brewery, and Neal's General Stores [N.O.R.A.] selling White Rose lamp oil. The pair of diamond patterned brick houses, Nos.24 & 26 are still there, but vacant and boarded up. Most of this view has disappeared including Spring's Café, just before the Star Inn, with its c1700 staircase and moulded handrail, demolished in 1980 [Mercantile Credit]. Some of the south side buildings have been re-built after the previous style or renovated.

27 c1905 The Pelican Inn Yard
"The famous Inn at Speenhamland, that stands below the hill, may well be called The Pelican, from its enormous bill"! So the old coaching-days rhyme goes — one of the foremost Inns on the London to Bath route. The "hoi-polloi" stayed here to visit the stars of the day performing at the Theatre just up the hill. Up to 60 coaches a day passed through Speenhamland in the late 1700's until the advent of the railway. By 1910 the Pelican coffee house yard was the headquarters of the Berkshire Yeomanry, 3rd Squadron (Newbury).
[Courtyard Office Block]

27

28

28 c1889 The Jubilee Clock
After weighty and heated deliberations the clock was erected as a memorial to the 50 years of Queen Victoria's reign (1887). It was unveiled by Mayor Cllr. Knight on March 4 1889, together with the Crimea Gun, the latter covered with the Union Jack and flanked by four local Crimea war veterans. Snow fell during the Ceremony which was also the first public performance of the Town Band. The clock, an eight-day Grahams dead-beat escapment, was made to the specifications of Stradling & Son. The ironwork was cast by George Smith of Glasgow & London and was decorated in gold and colours by Ravenor of Speenhamland. The day ended with the local worthies dining at the Chequers Hotel. From the ensuing caustic comments in the "NWN" some locals did not consider the clock a fitting memorial. In 1929 Mr. J.H. Godding donated funds for the present pillared structure.
Hall, previously Hall & Marsh, can be seen on the corner; the old established bookseller and printer was a meeting point for the folk living in Speenhamland. As a point of interest, a tall chimney can be seen behind Denners triple-gabled building, which had been demolished by the 1930s.
[Park Way]

29

29 November 1935 7/8 The Broadway
Willcock family
The triple-gabled 17th century building rebuilt in 1935 is shown during the 1935 election hustings. S.J. Willcock came to Newbury before World War I and took over the Broadway Dairy [La Riviera Restaurant], after the war moving to the present site. Mr. Willcock senior was true blue Tory but his son was of a different hue, a socialist. During the night some local Tory jokers fly-posted his shop windows with Clifton-Brown posters. As luck would have it the following morning the Tory candidate passed by in his car, was delighted to see his

posters and went into the shop and shook Mr. Willcock senior's hand effusively. Sidney Willcock, coming down from breakfast, heard and saw what had happened, was not at all amused, and proceeded to put his own "additions" on the posters. The joke back-fired on the Tories as he refused to remove the graffitied posters and had further pleasure in heckling the candidate at his local meetings. He died in 1955.

30

30 July 13 1899 "Lord" George Sanger's circus A lunch-time view up Northbrook Street, taken from a window of York House, and showing the crowds watching the circus progressing up the street. A traditional white-faced tragi-comedy clown can be seen in the last carriage. The previous Monday the circus had performed at Windsor Castle for Queen Victoria's grand-children. Notice the lamps as previously depicted in plate 28 have now been removed and four street-type lights are now erected on the road. The horse-trough in front of the Crimea Gun was provided by the Metropolitan Drinking Fountain & Cattle Trough Association in 1908, and is not shown in this book.

31

31 c1900 50 Northbrook Street Mrs. B. Webb In 1815 John Webb took over John Chapman's grocery business; he was succeeded by his son Thomas and then his two grandsons. One of them, Charles, could remember when tea was 8/- a pound and so expensive that only the rich could afford to buy it. He saw Newbury develop from a quiet town, with coaches the only means of news from outside, to the age of the train and telephone. The late 17th century building, tile-hung with three dormer windows, is much as it is to-day, their horse-drawn delivery waggon stands outside, the horse in a rough full clip, making his legs look as though they have woolly socks on. The centre shop window has a large display of Huntley & Palmer biscuits. The two Webb brothers are in the doorway, one of them wearing a mourning armband, a custom that has virtually died out in the south. [Wilbers]

32

32 c1900 Rear of J. Webb & Sons D. Roberts
A delightful and unusual photograph depicting the back of a long established grocer's shop. Even without people it tells a story of its own — the hanging delivery baskets and the barrow on a brick floor; trolley, water can, a bowl on the gravelled yard, a mop on the roof and above, old wooden guttering. On the left is a large cask with a spigot — containing mollasses maybe.

33 June 1887 Northbrook Street
Decorated for Queen Victoria's Jubilee — the main attraction at the time the photograph was taken seems to be the gentleman on the horse. Most of the shop blinds are down so the names cannot be seen. Alphonse Cary piano warehouse is next to Garlick the jeweller [Ladbrookes]. On the roadway facing the oncoming pony and trap is a young girl on an early tricycle. The group of folk on the right outside

33

Samuel Elliotts Albert Works entrance show a lad in a typical pre-1890 sailor suit with short knee-length trousers. The ladies outside Hamlins the tailor [Logan Cameras] are fashionably dressed with evidence of a bustle and their bonnets on the top of chignonned hair.

34 Whit-Monday, c1909 Horse Parade
Newbury Weekly News

Class I — a pair of carthorses owned by Mr. G.J. Cooper of Shaw Mills with J. Bartlett driving. The entrants gathered in Victoria Park and paraded up St. Mary's Road to the Broadway, down Northbrook and Bartholomew Streets, up St. John's and back down Cheap Street, the townsfolk enjoying the sight of anything up to 50 turnouts. Although the photographer is unknown one could well suspect it was J.W. Righton at No.42 [Visionhire]. The building is early Georgian in an unusual "Spanish Netherlands" style; the figure at the top left was one of four depicting the Four Seasons. Until recently the building had shrubs and tall weeds growing out of its roof, but is now more carefully preserved. Next door is C. Maggs the butchers [Trotmans]. The premises still has its disused abattoir at the rear and has been a butchers shop since before 1800.

34

35

36

37

35, 36, 37
J.W. Blacket & T.W. Turner 34 Northbrook Street Newbury Weekly News
In the 1840's the town's news appeared in the weekly Reading Mercury and the mid-week 1d. Berkshire Journal. The following summarises the difficult struggle to give birth to Newbury's own local newspaper:—
1854 H.J. Ashley of Bridge House — lasted six months
1859 Newbury Advertiser, James Blacket, abandoned after nine months of lone struggle
1867 February 7 — J. Walter Blacket & Thomas W. Turner started the Newbury Weekly News, one side printed in London with a circulation of 1200 and costing 1½d.
1868 The Crown, Henry Ford, Market Place — a few months
1870 Newbury Wonder, a four-page

newsheet by a Mr. House — it too died young
1873 "NWN" printed entirely locally at 1d., circulation 7000
1880 Newbury Advertiser — Liberal Party — short lived
1886 Newbury Express — Conservative Party, printed by Hall in the Broadway until 1890, and then at Reading until its demise in 1899
1910 Newbury Chronicle — lasted no more than five years.

The photographs show the two founders, and the presentation in 1933 to Alfred Collins who worked in the company from 1883. Seated left to right —
S.E. Scott, Ashley Turner, Alfred Collins, Mrs. T.W. Turner, Hugh Turner (Editor 1929-57), S.E. West, George Willis (Editor 1957-65).
Standing, left to right — C. Wood, S. Holley, R. Parker, G.H. Bullock, Miss M. Turner, V.E. Cooper, Miss K.M. Etherton, C.J. Barrett, Miss Thomas, F. Rolfe, G. Hughes, A.D. Prismall, Mrs. E.R. Fifield, S.V. Eastman, J.E. Russell, C.E.T. Scott, A.B. Williams, E.R. Fifield, B. Claridge, A. Purdue, J. Evans, W. Verney, H. Mills and A. West.

38 July 1933 Parade for the workless
Newbury District Museum
At a mass meeting in the Corn Exchange, Mayor Elsie Kimber proposed a scheme to provide work for Newbury's 800 unemployed. A Work Fund Scheme was already in operation paying a minimum of 35/- a week to a married man, (the union rate) for two existing council schemes — surfacing and draining of Wharf Road and Bear Lane, and extending the gas mains to Thatcham. To avoid the rates having to provide the funds, and local businesses thereby suffering, it was proposed all those employed should contribute 2d a week to the Scheme. The levelling and draining of Victoria Park was a future project costing £1,700, of which £1,100 should be paid for by the Work Fund Scheme.
The Newbury Volunteer Fire Brigade are seen in the Dennis pump outside Maison Stewart the hairdressers and Blandford the photographers, their shop fascias show the street is beginning to change its facade.

38

39

39 c1928 30 Northbrook Street R. Lambert
The Lamberts came from London during the first World War and took over Mrs. Oliver's confectionery shop. Alfred Lambert was well-known for his selection of fine pipe tobaccos and sundries. Pipes are being sold for 4/6d and 5/6d in the left window, quite expensive for those days, and the right window is heavily advertising Cadbury's chocolates. Two old gas lights, with the redundant lamps removed, hang over each window and four rows of glazed tiles give a neat finish to the double windowed symetrical shop front.
[James Walker & Son — in new Arcade]

40 c1890 Hopson & Sons, 28 Northbrook Street
Camp Hopson & Co. Ltd.
An intriguing interior of a shop selling second-hand furniture before the turn of the century. The windows and interiors of shops in those times were crammed with goods, the more displayed in the minimum of space the better. [James Walker & Son]

41 c 1903 Jack Hotel, 22 Northbrook Street
Named after "Jack" of Newbury, see plate 42. A hotel existed on the site from the mid-1750's. In the coaching days there was stabling at the rear of the premises and the local carriers for Beedon, Bucklebury, Chaddleworth, Frilsham, Hampstead-Norris, Hungerford, Leckhampstead and Shefford left the Jack in the 1840's. Horace Cadd was the last owner of the Hotel, he had a white cockatoo called Cocky who was sometimes known to speak "out of turn". Trade had declined substantially by 1935 and the site was sold and re-developed. The Hotel had its own named china from Henry Turner of Paddington — I have half a treasured egg cup with Jack Hotel, Newbury in a brown buckled circular belt printed on the bowl.
[Marks & Spencer]

40

41

42

42 c1913 23/24 Northbrook Street
Known as Jack of Newbury's house, the northern gable end seen here looking towards Stradling & Plenty [Tesco] is all that remains of the 15th century house. The house at one time had some wooden panels with the initials IW (John Winchcombe) and IS (John Smallwood). By 1883 these were in the possession of Walter Money no less, and by 1913 in Sudeley Castle at Winchcombe, the town from where John originated. John Smallwood, alias John Winchcombe entertained Henry VIII and Catherine of Aragon here in around 1518. He had 600 people working in what can be classed as the first factory in England, for the manufacture of wool into cloth, exporting to the Netherlands and elsewhere. It is said that Jack sent his own army of 100 Newburians to fight at Flodden field in 1513. There is no portrait known of Jack of Newbury, a Benefactor to the Parish Church, as was his son also named John, whose portrait hangs in Newbury District Museum. By 1736 the premises had been sub-divided into shops.

[Paiges]

43

43 c1906 10/11 Northbrook Street
During recent restoration work the gable pendants were found to be dated 1663 (not 1667, 8 or 9 as previously documented). This was the year that the then owner George Cowslade was Mayor and met his Monarch, Charles II, in August when he visited the local Civil War battlefields. The building is said in some works to have been the *first* meeting house of the Baptists in 1640 but this could not be if the fine Carolean building was not erected until some 20 years later. However, it is quite probable the Baptists used a room in the building that was previously on the same site and continued to meet in the depicted building. In the 1600's all or part of the site was an Inn called The George.

[Camp Hopson & Co. Ltd.]

44

44 c1906 Northbrook Street looking south
On the right is Hannibal Hill [Hepworths] who sold overcoats for one guinea in 1909. His metal open-work sign is seen in reverse. It was removed by 1911, but some early postcard printers used to obliterate the sign from negatives prior to printing. Toomers can be seen at No.4, previously the Crown Inn, and Fielders the chemist at Nos.2/3. By 1928 Toomers had moved to Nos.2/3 and Timothy Whites were at Nos.4/5. At No.1 Liddiards [Town Bookseller] remains much the same to-day, except that the decorative ironwork balcony was removed many years ago as it become unsafe. This premises was a butchers shop from at least 1794. As ever, the Town Hall clock somehow manages to get its face in the picture, although I suspect many photographers went to some length to see it was included if at all possible.

45

45 c1900 Bridge Street Griffin & Sons
Charles Saunders established a pork butcher and fruit shop on Newbury Bridge in 1856. By the mid-1880's, the business had been taken over by G. Griffin, who built up a remarkable reputation for pork sausages made on the premises, as they are to-day. When the Racecourse was opened in 1905 many of the visitors used to stop off in Northbrook Street to buy lardy cakes at Staples and sausages from Griffin's. The windows are dressed out with a variety of porcine delicacies: chops, bacon, pies at 1/8d and the like. A carcase and a half hangs in the doorway. The delivery boy with his basket stands ready to make the local deliveries in the horse-drawn trap; a whip is propped against the seat.

46

46 c1903 Mansion House and Shambles
The building is said to have been built in 1742 by John Clarke, whose workshops occupied the site behind Cheap Street which was later used by Plenty's. On the first floor of the Mansion House were a suite of rooms suitable for assemblies. The open arched "Shambles" underneath were originally used by butchers and then for the sale of butter, poultry, and the like. In this picture a Chief Inspector stands with a constable outside the Shambles prior to its demolition in 1909 in order to allow free movement of traffic in Mansion House Street. The building was sometimes referred to as the Old Town House or Mansion House.

47 1909 Demolition of the Shambles
Newbury District Museum
A marvellous photograph, one of six taken during the demolition work. The size of the Mansion House can now be realised. The work is also going on the other side of the standing first floor back brick wall, as a ladder is propped up against it. The Town Hall, with its distinctive clock tower, was built in 1878-81 designed by John Money (Walter Money's brother). It is now undergoing extensive internal reconstruction into office suites.
"Batty" Wheeler had moved from Cheap Street to Mansion House Street a year earlier than previously recorded — his paintwork in the photograph certainly looks very new. In front of the White Hart

47

Hotel in the distance is a large pile of timber or bricks, a horse and cart pass up Mansion House Street, against the traffic to our minds, followed by a policeman. The old man at the corner of the demolished building appears to be almost a classic example of "leaning on one's shovel"!

48

48 June 22 1911 Mansion House Street

Mrs. J. Camp

Processing to the Parish Church for King George V's Coronation Thanksgiving service. The local councillors, followed by the macebearers precede the Mayor, Cllr, Alfred Camp, with Rev. L. Majendie Rector, Parish Church, alongside him. The photograph was originally owned by Alfred Camp, who came to Newbury from Devon in 1886 and took over James & Bodman's drapery business at 8/9 Northbrook Street. The newly completed Town Hall is flanked with crowds, including some of the Town Band standing on the wooden paved street in their smart new military type uniform. A couple of local lads, one with a handful of cabbage plants, both with crates of beer, are no doubt off to their West Mills allotments. The Mayor looks at them perhaps wistfully — it was a week of continual social events for both him and his wife; they departed a few days later for a well-earned holiday on the Isle of Wight.

49

49 November 7 1902 Opening of the Cloth Hall

Newbury District Museum

The Museum was originally at the Literary & Scientific Institute [Brook House] in Northbrook Street. The Cloth Hall had been the south wing of the old Corporation cloth factory, built in 1627 but by 1726 used as a grain stores. Cllr. John Rankin (Mayor 1899-1901) initiated a scheme in 1901 to restore the neglected building as a memorial to the late Queen Victoria. The scene depicted here shows Mayor Rankin, who performed the opening ceremonies, flanked by the macebearers and accompanied by the architect Francis Mount and other dignitaries, with the Volunteer Fire Brigade providing their usual guard of honour. The weather was kind for November, many more of the townsfolk attended than was expected, including two loose dogs. The proceedings were followed by a sumptuous luncheon at the Town Hall supplied by the Dolphin Hotel. The Museum has had five Honorary curators, a full-time professional Curator being appointed in 1978.

50

50 c1890 Dolton's Barn in the Wharf
Berkshire Archeological Society

Dolton's the corn merchants were established by 1845. Their storage barn at the north-west corner of the Wharf has obscure origins; it is an unusual structure incorporating a double ridge, which can be seen behind the open roofed front. The group in the centre of the building include a typical local farm waggon, the smaller cart harnessed to a donkey, essential transport in many rural areas. The date the barn was demolished cannot be definitely stated, but it disappeared in the mid-1920's and is understood to have been re-erected in the United States. The white Volunteer Fire Brigade building can be seen to the left of the barn.

51 1898 The Wharf J. Stradling

A photograph of some of Newbury's early motor enthusiasts in the Wharf, taken before 1904 since none of the cars have licence plates. From left to right:
Kathleen Plenty with her father in a Benz, then Stradling & Plenty's foreman Charley Pearce on a tricycle, probably a de Dion Bouton. The two people in a steam brake or van are not known. The vehicle, however, is most unusual and was made by Brown & May of Devizes, although they specialised in traction engines. Next are an unknown couple on a most unsafe looking quadricycle, possibly an Ariel, and finally come George Cosburn of the Caxton Printing Works and James Stradling in another Benz.

51

52

53

52 September 29 1892 Volunteer Fire Brigade
S. Thomas

The Newbury VFB was founded in 1878 after a disastrous fire in Church lane [Arcade]. Previously, the Borough Engine House was on Bridge Street and the fire escape was located under the Town Hall. Before then the engine was kept near the Parish Church. The Brigade is shown here before setting off to Highclere Castle with the Shand Mason pump engine. Their dog Bruno is in the foreground; he apparently spent much time outside a Bartholomew Street butcher's window "thoughtfully contemplating the joints", but when the firebell rang disappeared fast to follow "his" crew. Some delay was caused in attending fires as the Volunteers first had to catch the horses, either down on Northcroft or in The Marsh.

— Impey. & H. Bottle on the horses H. Hannington. R. Freebody. C. Bravant. C. Adey back row of pump.

E. Harrison. J. Hassell. T. Langton front row of pump.

H. Biddis. J. Pearce between wheels. H. Church (Captain) behind wheels. S. White. G. Booth behind ladder. Bruno the dog by front wheel.

53 October 1930 NVFB Dennis Pump
Mrs. J. Camp

The new Dennis fire pump depicted here at the Wharf Station, replaced a 17 year old engine and was purchased by public donations, enabling the Brigade to be more mobile. It may not be fully realised the service which these unpaid Volunteers gave, not only to Newbury and the surrounding area, but as far away as Southampton, Exeter, and Bristol during World War II. Three Newbury Volunteers lost their lives, and four were injured in 1941 on a blitz call-out to the South Coast. The Brigade ceased to exist in April 1942 when the National Fire Service started, many of the Volunteers joining it.

H.J. Hassall, J. Spracklen standing in front of the ladder at the back.

J. Brindley by the rear wheel, with A. Turner standing on the rear step of the pump.

C. New, A. Allin, J. Crocker, F. Seward and B. Miles the back row on the pump.

J. Wheeler, B. Camp, N. Monen and R. Green sitting on the front of the pump.

J. Heath at the wheel.

C. Rummings standing by E. Martin (Captain).

54

55

54 c1910 The Granary
Chosen to illustrate the original use of the Granary. A couple of full grain sacks can be seen stacked up against the building, and the nearby grainstore door is open. The door where the man is standing is approximately the present day entrance to the Tourist office. The timber framed overhanging first floor was approached by a flight of somewhat dangerous looking treads alongside three steps. Sack trucks are stood at the far end of the building before the neat wooden paling of John Flint's coal yard. In 1933, the ground floor was renovated and turned into shops, then allowed to regress somewhat. Part of the ground floor is again shops, the first floor now completely opened up to provide more Museum display area and offices.

55 c1928 Norton's Bus Service — Newbury/Thatcham P. Hassell
One of the many rural bus services of the 1920's, Nortons had their Depot at 13 West Mills [Boultons Yard]. Jim Lawrence at the wheel and William Titcomb the conductor. On the wall outside Dreweatt, Watson & Barton is an advertisement for the sale of Jewells Farm at Bucklebury. Some of the other bus services of the time were Denham's, Reliance, Venture, Pioneer (on Thursdays only to St. Mary Bourne), Thackerays, Austins, Howletts, "The Doris" to Wash Common, and Durnfords. Some also ran day excursion buses — even as far as Brighton. Most were eventually absorbed into the Thames Valley Traction Co:, now Alder Valley.

56

57

58

59

60

Some faces from the 1850's

56 Mrs. William Penford, whose husband owned the drapery business at 13/14 Northbrook Street. The soft pleats of her dress are a feature of 1840's and 50's dresses.

57 Mr. Joseph Fuller of Goldwell Park, the only "manor house" in the Parish, built for William le Marchant in the 1740's. Mr. Fuller lived there c1848-64.

58 The three Blacket Boys. The eldest, Walter, started the Newbury Weekly News in 1867

59 Robert Long, "the boy next door". His parents had a glass & china shop in Northbrook Street in the late 1850's. He was Mayor in 1889 and 1896.

60 Mrs. Charles or Henry Dolton, wife of one of the Dolton brothers, corn and seed merchants of Speenhamland and the Wharf.

61 June 21 1887 Queen Victoria's Jubilee
Newbury District Museum

The day commenced with the Russian Gun being fired in the Marsh at 6.00 in the morning, again at 11.00 to commence the procession, and finally at 1.00pm to start the dinner. There is a vast concourse of people as far as the eye can see, in this pair of photographs taken within an hour of each other, hence the slight confusion in the middle where parasols and people do not quite match. The right hand photograph depicts a carriage carrying four top-hatted local worthies and a Scot in full dress seated beside the driver arriving at the Town Hall followed by another carriage.

The left hand photograph shows, in the foreground, one of the 23 tables set up for the local children who consumed an incredible 1500 lbs. of meat, a ton of plum pudding and 300 gallons of ginger beer and lemonade! The left-overs were distributed

61

to those who had applied, some having walked miles into Newbury from their outlying villages. One lady caused great confusion by "imprudently venturing to sit" on one of the tables which promptly collapsed along with those already seated. All the main streets were decorated and held their own dinners — 650 people in Bartholomew Street alone.

One amusing parade during the day was a late afternoon demonstration by dog owners with their dogs in regulation muzzles, but draped in crepe as a protest against a recent prosecution against an unmuzzled dog.

The day ended with illuminations in the main streets and it was recorded that drunks were "exceedingly small" although free beer was being served throughout the day.

62

62 c1899 Market Day Sansome & George
The stalls are erected and goods displayed; there is a cluster of locals, many of them ladies, one pushing a hooded pram, and a man manoeuvering an empty barrow towards a waiting cart drawn by a grey horse with maybe planks propped up on the cart side. In the distance the stalls stretch away to Bear Lane. The waggons on the right, opposite the Queens Hotel, present an almost solid line of traffic, but as the horses and traps are passing them, they could well be stationary carriers waiting for the Market to close. One would imagine from the shadows that it is around 3.00-4.00pm in the autumn, as everyone looks well wrapped up. Notice the large ornate street light, erected in December 1855 and first lit on Christmas Eve, the focal point of the Market Place, soon to be replaced in 1903 by Queen Victoria's Statue, on the approximate site of the old Market Cross which had gone by 1828 along with the old Guildhall.

63

63 June 10 1901 Return of the Boer War Veterans R.L.Gibbs
The volunteers arrived at the Railway Station wearing their khaki uniform and South African campaign medals. The carriage containing Colonel Ricardo was drawn by the members of the NVFB to the town's Welcome in the Market Place. 14 volunteers from Newbury served in the 39th & 58th Berkshire Yeomanry (and a further 5 from the district), four had been invalided home and two were still in Africa. The photograph shows the Mayor, Cllr. Rankin, with sable-trimmed gown and mayoral chain to the right of the lamp post, with his Address in his left hand, surrounded by civic dignitaries. It is probably Colonel Ricardo shaking hands with Lt. Giles Ayres who had been invalided home, the incident recorded in the "NWN" with touching acclamation by the crowd. The NVFB volunteers can be seen in front of the carriage, the following carriage horses pulling the Veterans with one of the Berkshire Imperial Yeomanry astride the lead horse.
On July 9 a public dinner was held at the Corn Exchange with Major-General Earl Dundonald, who had been at the relief of Ladysmith, as guest of honour.

64

64 June 24 1903 Unveiling Queen Victoria's Statue Newbury District Museum
Donated by "Lord" George Sanger, one of Newbury's more colourful sons. He was born the son of a Moonraker (Wiltshireman) who had been press-ganged onto HMS Victory at the Battle of Trafalgar, wounded, and then discharged on a pension. In the summer months father and son toured the fairs with a peep show. George's first public performance was at the 1838 Coronation Fete in Hyde Park. He had a flair for teaching animals tricks and trained a pair of hares to box, fire off guns and beat tambourines, and took £50 in one day. Later he leased the Agricultural Hall in London and sometimes took £2000 in a day. His daughter Mrs. Reeve unveiled the 38 foot statue, which had been made at the Royal Doulton Potteries. The NVFB, as ever, formed a guard of honour, the Town Band played, the Mayor, Cllr. Day, and civic dignitaries attended, and the ceremony was followed by a lunch at the Town Hall. "Lord" George is seated by the standing Macebearer, the press are busy taking notes, one even sitting down on the official steps!
Within 30 years the statue was moved to Greenham House gardens as it prevented the free movement of traffic. Her Majesty now stands ignominiously on half her pedestal in Victoria Park, guarded with only a pair of lions; the other pair were given to the Child-Beale Trust at Pangbourne for some reason or other.

65

65 1906 Newbury Town Band G. Collier
Their first performance was at the unveiling of the Broadway Jubilee clock in 1889. They are seen here wearing their early type uniform of braided jacket and pillbox hat. This postcard was sent by F.H.H. (Higgs, a shopkeeper in York Road), to Charles Bosley at Shaw reminding him to attend Thursday's band practice. The bandmaster was a Mr. Eggleton, and other players were Messrs. Rodd, Dell, Biddis, Williams, Pearce, Spracklen, and Watkins.
In the background behind Queen Victoria's statue is the premises of A.W. Purdue [William & Glyn's Bank] mealmen, who also hired out horses and traps. They were an old Newbury family tracing their descent from John West (1640-1724) the man responsible for Christ's Hospital Gift foundation. Next door is the Kings Arms [Plaza], Wells & Sons spirit and wine merchants, and George Cosburn's house next to the Corn Exchange.
[Hatchet Hotel]

66 c1907 Kings Arms Hotel
The proprieter Jack Milsom is probably the gentleman in the doorway behind one of his advertised gigs, a little terrier dog sitting on the driver's seat. Prior to 1780 it was called the Waggon & Horses, and before that The White Lion. It was bought by Jimmy Tufnail in 1925 and re-built as the Plaza Theatre with an arcade of shops. Tufnail, an eccentric character who died in 1930, became a councillor so he could, in his own words, oppose them! The Plaza was taken over by the Council in 1933 and used for plays and the like. By 1979 the structure needed repairs costing £35,000 and was recently sold to Dreweatt, Watson & Barton. Oddly, the proposed facade for the ground and first floors is not unlike the original Kings Arms (see Plate 64)

The
KING'S ARMS
WINE & SPIRIT JACK MILSOM. MERCHANT.
HARNESS HORSES & COBS ON HIRE.
MARKET ORDINARY FROM 12·30 TO 2-30
BILLIARDS AND POOL.
HUNTERS & HACKS FOR SALE OR HIRE.

66

DYERS
PICKFORD

67

68

67 June 21 1911 Market Place S. Pocock
This photograph was taken the day before the festivities for King George V's Coronation — the clock gives the time as 10.10am and folk are in their work-day clothes — a scratching dog adding character to the scene! It is hardly surprising the decorations had to be in place by at least the day before; it must have taken hours of planning and physical effort to produce such displays. Some of the greenery used came from the Highclere Estate. The Pickford Company, one of whose horse-drawn carts is parked outside the Queens Hotel, was owned by Mr. Baxendale of Greenham Lodge. This picture is one of a pair of sepia-toned photographs numbered on the back '15' & '16' — a record of 1-14 would be fascinating.

68 August 1887 Newbury Amateur Orchestral Union
The NAOU, one of the oldest amateur orchestras in the country, was founded by Messrs. Toms, Staples, Eatwell, Seymour, Biddis, & Mathews, with G.H. Bates as the first conductor in 1879, from a "scratch" orchestra conjured together for a Volunteer Fire Brigade function.
Pictured here at a charity performance in Southend-on-Sea are:
Back row, left-right: Bishop, double bass. Boy Helper. H Brown, 1st violin. H. Curtis, 2nd violin. J. Guyer, 2nd violin. J. Augard, 1st clarinet. J. Stradling, 2nd clarinet. Thomas, flute. Bowering, collector.
Front row left-right: J. Brown, cello. J.H. Hopson, bassoon. E. Staples, viola. and Gamble, cornet.

69 October 22/23 1888 Interior of the Corn Exchange Mrs. F.W. Titcomb
The inside of the Corn Exchange, decorated out with great ingenuity to simulate an old English Market by the Baptist Church, to raise funds for the renovation of their church and an extension to the school in Northbrook Street. The Baptist church started locally in 1640, their own meeting house was erected in Northcroft Lane in 1702. In 1859 a church and school was erected in Northbrook Street [Richard Shops]. The new school was opened on its present St. Mary's Hill site in 1934, fulfilling a double-duty as the church in Northbrook Street had been vacated and the new one next to the new school was undergoing construction.

69

70 c1900 The Andrews Brothers Mrs. K. Fisher
Newbury Cycling Club was formed in 1877, with its headquarters at the Queens Hotel. The inaugural ride was to Hungerford, the members wearing grey serge uniforms and pill-box hats. The first advertisement in the "NWN" by a cycle dealer was that of Smart & Sons of Cheap Street in 1877. Around 1888 the prototype of the modern bike started to appear in Newbury and the craze for cycling started. The photograph depicts (front to rear) H.J., F.J. & C.W. Andrews, well-known local cycling brothers, who were known to travel as far as Brighton on their "tri-bike". Their mother was a marvellous cook and helped run Staples (caterers and pastrycooks) at 32, Northbrook Street with her sister and brother-in-law Mr. & Mrs. John Staples.

70

71

71 c1914 W.H. Giles – Newbury Carrier
Harry Giles is seen here outside the demolished Wesleyan chapel in Charnham Street, Hungerford. He, and his father before him, were one of the vital links with the outlying districts. Their cart, and later van, left the Queens Hotel on Tuesdays & Fridays for Marsh Benham/ Kintbury/Hungerford and Thursdays and Saturdays direct to Hungerford. These dedicated carriers (and there were some 60 going from Newbury to London, Farnham, Portsmouth, Southampton and local villages in 1844) were the life-line of the rural communities. They carried the mails (sometimes illegally!), medicines, parcels, messages, animals, and people. They were marooned in snowdrifts and almost drowned in flooded fords. Their devotion to their community cannot be calculated in this age of the motor car.

72

73

72 c1903 Market Place
On the right, by the turning to Bear Lane, is the Bear Inn owned by Strange's Aldermaston Brewery. The building was demolished in 1961. A group of men are outside George Cosburn's Caxton Printing works, and next door is the Carnarvon Arms [Barclays Bank plc] the large roundel presumably showing the Carnarvon family arms. The Queens Hotel lies alongside the Corn Exchange. The view north is dominated by the London & Counties Bank, an Italian Gothic building by Chancellor in 1864 [National Westminster Bank plc]. To the right is the part-17th century Waggon & Horses, to the left Beynons. Note on the left the Co-op. building with its first and second floor symetrical windows, the first floor ones combined into two large ones in 1908. At the time of writing a demolition order has just been granted and the building will shortly disappear forever.

73 November 1927 Brighton Car Rally
H. Butcher
Alfred Hollands of Greenham Mill, with his son Arthur in a 3½hp single cyclinder red and black Benz photographed before (or maybe after) taking part in the first Commemoration Brighton car rally. Alfred Hollands purchased the Benz new in 1900, ran it for some seven years, then stored it. The car was registered again in 1927 and after a few minor renewals, rewiring of ignition and change of plugs, it started after a couple of pulls at the flywheel. Arthur Hollands drove the car from London to Brighton in 4 hours 26 minutes (with three stops for carburetter flooding) for which he was awarded a gold medal. His father followed behind in his own car. On returning to Newbury the car gave a charity demonstration for the Hospital and was also given permission to drive round the interior of the Corn Exchange! The Benz is now green and has an honoured place in the Birmingham Museum of Science and Industry.
This photograph was taken at the corner of Bear Lane. Robert Martin's harness business and Danford Skinners, Outfitters, are in the background.

74

74 November 1914 Bear Lane Smithy H. Butcher
For 99 years three generations of the Butcher family were farriers and blacksmiths at Bear Lane. The photograph depicts the founder Frederick far left, his son Vince with folded arms, and Army horses from the Racecourse Camp. The smithy was forced to close in 1961, just a few months short of their centenary, when Bear Lane was widened.
I can still clearly recall Vince's son Henry shoeing the docile coal merchant's cart horses, whereas my horse's favourite trick was to bite his behind! The smell of burning hooves, flying red-hot sparks, Henry with a couple of shoeing nails in his mouth, and still able to talk, hammer banging on anvil, lives on in the memory.
[Barclays Bank car park]

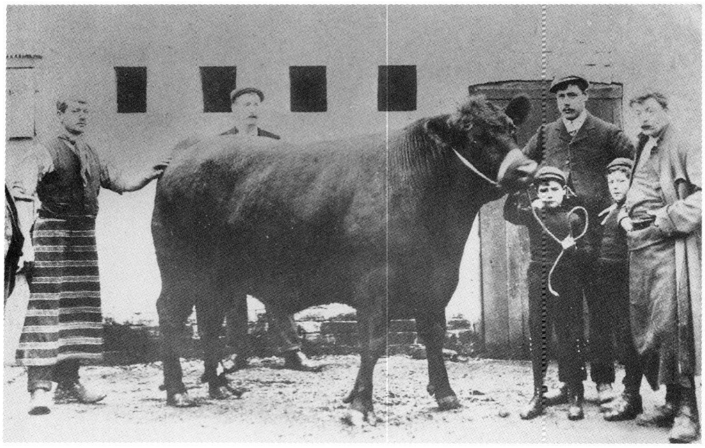

75

75 c1908 Council Abattoir Mrs. G. King
It was situated behind the Corn Exchange in the Bear Lane area. This photograph was taken as an advertisement card for Tom Randall Senior, seen in front of the door with two of his three sons. Tom Laidler of Boundary Road is partly hidden behind the bull's hindquarters. At that time Tom Randall lived in Stanley Road and had his butchers shop in Bartholomew Street.
Until the early 1960's, the Corporation abattoir leased units to butchers who did not have their own facilities. The slaughter of animals for human consumption is a difficult area to research because nothing of any substance has ever been written; presumably folk were squeamish as to how the meat "arrived" in the butcher's window. Notice the high windows to prevent passers-by being able to see into the slaughterhouse.

77

76

78

76 c1902 General Post Office Newbury District Museum

77 c1927 Mr G. Tomkins: Rural Postman Mrs. S. Marsh

78 c1935 Mr E. Taylor: Telegram Boy E. Taylor

The present GPO in Cheap Street was opened in 1896. After 1840, the GPO was variously in Northbrook Street at Nos.9, 86, & 105 [Camp Hopson, Cordings, Bridge House] and in Mansion House Street. The earliest town mark for Newbury is recorded in 1742; the postmaster in 1800 being responsible for Thatcham, Woolhampton, Chieveley, Kintbury, Kingsclere, and Ilsley mail receiving offices.

George Tomkins is in the old type jaunty crowned cap with the GPO badge over the brim, his delivery bag over the shoulder.

Ernie Taylor started as a telegraph boy and by his retirement in 1981 was in charge of the main sorting office. His telegram pouch can be seen affixed to his belt. Telemessages sent through the mail are just not the same as the old Telegram in its distinctive envelope delivered by a young lad on a motor-bike.

79

80

79 c1890 Plenty's Eagle Iron Works
Museum of English Rural Life
Founded by 1790 by William Plenty, a wheelwright from Southampton. He designed and built a Patent Plough in 1800, and the first Lifeboat in 1816. The Company produced agricultural equipment, and also ironwork for the Kennet & Avon Canal including a bridge near Thatcham. The family lived over the works in Cheap Street and William's son, Edward, was Mayor in 1865. The Company moved to Hambridge Lane in 1965. The photograph is difficult to accurately date but was quite possibly taken for the firm's centenary. The man perched on the roof was an amusing feature of quite a few commemorative-type photographs of the Victorian era.
[North portion Mall complex/Ravenseft Phase I]

80 c1900 Plenty's Eagle Iron Works
W.G. Smith
The gang who had worked on order No.7654, the chalked number on the top right section, a marine boiler with the Company's plate affixed on the left side. Notice the foreman in the front with the pair of dividers, the gang with their tools, hammers, chisels, sledge hammer; and the two lads in the middle who are possibly apprentices. The marine division was formed in 1863 and by 1903 the boiler section had moved to Kings Road, exporting to all parts of the British Empire.

81

The parent company merged with Sigmund Pulsometer Pumps of Reading in 1969.

81 c1908 Cheap Street looking south

82 1935 Alderman John Rankin

Newbury District Museum

McIlroy & Rankin, outfitters and drapers founded by 1898, is on the left at No.42 with its hanging gas lamps [Newdays (vacant)]. Next door is Freeman, Hardy & Willis one of Newbury's plethora of boot and shoe suppliers. Opposite at No.29, Greens newsagents with a hanging paper rack outside, the white Metropolitan Bank, and then Bell & Sons, competitor's of John Rankin's store.
John Rankin, shown here in 1935 when he was made the first Honorary Freeman of the Borough, was an old Newburian who was Mayor three times. He was instrumental in the renovation of the Cloth Hall in 1902 and a much respected citizen. In 1955 John Rankin Junior and Infant schools were named after him.

83 June 21 1887 25-28 Cheap Street B. Moore Johnsons grocery shop, previously W. Joplen, stands decorated for Queen Victoria's Jubilee, the first-floor garlands spelling "VICTORIA", the fascia decorated with greenery, garlands, and paper lanterns. A young lad in fashionable boater and watchchain stands at the entrance to Falkland Place, so named because Lord Falkland is said to have spent the night and taken Communion in a room behind No.25 before the first Battle of Newbury. The white painted Diamond Tap and Brewery is just after the entrance to the old Cattle Market. All were demolished in Ravenseft Phase I in 1970. [Trents-Cordon Bleu]

82

83

84

84 c1910 Interior of No.53 Cheap Street

J. Gould

The photograph is a trifle faded, but offers a rare glimpse into the interior of a grocer's shop. Stephen Gould started the business in 1827, his son is shown here on the left. No advertising opportunity was lost either inside or on the outer fascia — Epp's Cocoa, Van Houten's cocoa (no brand loyalty here), Bovril, and Hudsons. Packets of tea fill the top left hand shelves and other goods are neatly stacked in the compartments. The paper cones which one of the staff is holding were used to put dry goods in, such as pulses and dried fruits, made on the spot in seconds by the staff deftly rolling the paper from its bottom point and turning over the top point when full.

FAMILIES

85

The
NEW MARKET
INN.
MARTIN'S
MOTOR &
CYCLE WORKS
ROLFE
50
THE WELCOME
DINING &
TEA ROOMS
GOOD BEDS
2630. Cheap St.

86

85 c1870 Cheap Street

Newbury Library, now in Newbury District Museum

One of the few early photographs of one of Newbury's three main streets, seen before Market Street was opened in 1872. P.(eter) Al(len)'s short-lived Brewery (1869-76) can be seen at the corner of Gashouse Lane [Kings Road West], so called as the gasworks opened in 1826 were just along the lane behind Turk's Brass and Iron foundary [Foebel] on the opposite corner. The pillar box and gas lamp are sited where the Public Library is now; on the opposite side of the street stood St. Mary's Almhouses, rebuilt in 1864. The two light coloured houses where the pair of carts is passing were demolished to open up Market Street, although there was a small lane through to Bartholomew Street. The newly completed Parish Church pinnacles can just be seen over the roof tops.

As in the following plate, the triple gables of the old Merriman family house (c1679) [Penns] stand out, followed by the old Catherine Wheel before it was rebuilt as we know it to-day.

86 c1908 Cheap Street

A well know view of Cheap Street but it stands repeating. The Newmarket Inn, built in c1869, just prior to the new Cattle Market opening, and as far as Penns shoe shop at No.33 with its triple gables, have all been demolished. The crenellated Catherine Wheel at No.35 still stands, the long time footpath for the populace through to Bartholomew Street now blocked off. The east side of Cheap Street seen here has not changed that much. The paved Market Street or crossing point should be noted; it is now the entrance to a car park.

87 June 28 1905 Public Library

A public library had been mooted in 1886, however it was not until 1905 that the foundation stone was laid by Mrs. Eleanor Palmer, seen here with the Mayor, Frederick Hopson, Rev. Dangerfield, and the Rural Dean on her right. F.C. Mackarness (Liberal MP for Newbury 1906-10) is second from the right in front of the flag with the Rev. Titchmarsh. Built by Hoskings Brothers on ground previously used as the work house, the original book stock of 18,000 volumes came from donations and the Library of the old Literary & Scientific Institute. Not until 1926 was the borrower able to browse among the shelves, the books were selected from a printed list. The first librarian, a Mr. Rosling, was known to rigidly censor any book he considered might corrupt local morals. He was succeeded by Helen Purvis

87

in 1940 who retired in 1974 after 35 years in Newbury Library.
Incidentally, it may look as though the occasion was marred by rain, however the ladies are shielding their faces from the sun.

88 c1898 13/14 Cheap Street
Attwells were competitors of Griffins on the Bridge, but not for long, for by World War I Armstrongs had taken over Attewells, followed within two years by W.H. Gibby. Attewells also sold dairy products, cooked meats, and poultry. The windows are dressed out with tempting goods, the usual carcases hanging outside. Mrs. Attewell in addition ran a refreshment room and lodging house. St. Mary's Almhouses (opposite the Public Library) can just be seen to the right, demolished with Nos. 13/14 in 1971. [9-14 Mill Reef House (late Council offices)].

89 c1935 9-12 Cheap Street Mrs. F.W Titcomb
This photograph was taken prior to the buildings being demolished in 1936. A.W. Neate's high roof can be seen at No.8 on the left, then come Durnford & Son who ran bus excursions in the 20's & 30's. Cuffs the butcher, with cobwebs behind the first floor windows, is closed down and moved. In the entrance to Princes Place, with its trussed arch, is a large black wooden board stating the times of the services at the new Baptist school, where services were being held prior to the church being erected. Mr. Sturgess the hairdresser at No.11 advertises he has moved to 100 Bartholomew Street and Elsie Foster at No.12 has also gone.

88

89

90

90 June 1897 7 Cheap Street Midwinters Ltd
By 1830, John Shaw was trading as seedsman, corn merchant, and market gardner on the Cheap Street site. When Shaw moved to London in 1860, Charles Midwinter (sixth from right) took over the corn dealing side and in 1880 erected the present building. Charles being Congregationalist and Temperance would not sell malting barley; his son Henry (fourth from right) was of the same religious convictions but had a more entrepreneurial nature and did sell malting barley. Edwin, Charles's grandson, (first left in the window) duly succeeded to the business; the present Chairman is the founder's great, great grandson.

91 1903 Cheap Street
The turning to the railway station is on the left with an advertisement for Simmons dated Michaelmas 1903. Giles the confectioner is at No.3 [Motorists Discount Centre], the Pigeons Inn with a hanging gas lamp at No.5, the large tree is the far side of Midwinters. On the east side you can see the chequered brickwork of Nos.69/70 next to the Sun Inn with a three-wheeled milk handcart, followed by the lower building of Nos.65/8, then the bow-front windows at No.63 [Chivers] alongside the horse and

91

cart. The Axe & Compass at No.73 is not seen here, but many will recall the building before it was demolished along with all the others on the right as far as No.63 to accomodate the Ring Road in 1961. In the foreground are a couple of Gordon Boys, whose headquarters at this time was in Princes Place. The scheme was started in Newbury in 1894 by the local gentry to relieve youth unemployment; they cleaned windows, chopped wood, delivered parcels etc. and were a familiar local sight until World War I.

92 1904 74 Cheap Street J. Wheeler
The cycle business was founded about 1902 by Edward C. Wheeler (affectionately known as "Batty", which he certainly wasn't).
Previously he had been employed as a Borough mechanic and he repaired cycles in his spare time. "Batty" is seen here behind the motorcyles, BL 354 a Rex cycle registered to Harden of Woodspeen on March 12, and BL 419 a 3hp Ormonde registered to himself on May 9, 1904. The Company moved to the (present) Midland Bank site in 1909, The Broadway in 1918, and London Road in 1957. No.74 became Jimmy Tufnail's cinema which opened in October 1910, by which time Nos.75/6, seen in the photograph after the entrance to Golding's Yard, and Nos.77/79, had been demolished.

93 1935 Railway Goods Yard J. Gould
John Gould and his father's "Betsy", outside the GWR Goods yard with the cart neatly loaded with parcels just collected. Two of the houses and gardens of Jubilee Road can be seen the far side of the railway track. John Gould has devoted nearly 40 years to the preservation, conservation, and maintenance of the Kennet & Avon Canal and is a familiar sight to-day in Newbury, come rain or shine, in wellies and duffle coat, his collie Barney not far away! [Ring road/Berkshire Builders]

92

93

94

95

94 April 4 1898 Inauguration of the Lambourn Valley Railway
Museum of English Rural Life

A tramline link to Lambourn was suggested in 1873 and within a year a mile of tramway track had been laid from Cheap Street to Donnington Square; the project was then abandoned. A Bill for the railway link was passed through Parliament in 1883, however financial problems beset the scheme from the outset. After innumerable difficulties the line eventually opened for traffic in 1898.

The photograph shows No.1384 locomotive (at Lambourn Station)owned by the GWR and loaned to the LVR line. It was built by Sharp Stewart in early 1876 for the Watlington & Princes Risborough Railway, and is a 2-4-0 side tank type with 4′ coupled wheels and a tall dome, the tank capacity being 480 gallons. She was rebuilt in November 1898 and sold to the Bute Works Supply Company in 1911, and later became No.4 "Hesperus" on the Weston, Clevedon & Portishead Railway. She was finally cut up in 1937.

The line was officially opened by the MP for Berkshire, Mr. W.G. Mount. It was taken over by the GWR in May 1905, and closed in 1960 except for a short-lived goods service to RAF Welford.

95 1905 LVR/GWR Railmotor Newbury Library

After trials in 1902 the GWR decided to build a number of railmotors for suburban and branch lines. The photograph shows No.1, built in October 1903 as a 52 seater, 57 feet long, as used on the Lambourn Valley line after its acquisition by the GWR in 1905. It had an internal partition, with a smoking compartment at the engine end (far end in this photograph). The vertical external matchboard sides were painted chocolate and cream, and 10cwt. of coat was carried in a bunker in the boiler compartment. Railmotors were gradually superseded by Auto-trains, No.1 being withdrawn from service in 1914.

Newbury water tower is in the background and Blackboys bridge beyond, on the right Nos.81/3 Bartholomew Street [Ellora Tandoori/E.C. Paine].

96

96 c1905 Newbury Station
The GWR line to Newbury (& Hungerford) was opened in 1847. This is a common photograph, but is shown again to afford a comparision with plate 116. The large wooden sign shows Newbury as a more important junction station than it certainly is now. The engine is a 2-4-0 type, numbered between 3232 and 3251, built at Swindon during 1892/3, a development of the 2201 class. It was superseded at the turn of the century by the more powerful 4-4-0 class and relegated to secondary routes in the London and Bristol areas before being withdrawn in 1930. Behind the engine is a passenger luggage van with clerestory coaches following. Between the guard and wooden seat a gas lamp can be seen, a common item on a country platform, with milk churns tucked into the corner by the Epp's Cocoa advertisement sign. Away in the background is the Blackboys Bridge.

97

97 August 1899 East Newbury from the air
D.W. Liddiard
A very early aerial photograph taken from Rev. J.M. Bacon's gas balloon which had just taken off from the new Gas Works sited in Kings Road (previously behind Cheap Street). Boundary Road stretches away in a near straight line to Greenham Mill; a crowd of upturned faces watches the balloon drift away towards Enborne. The Railway line and yard are in the mid-foreground, the spur of the Didcot/Newbury line can be seen joining the GWR track at Greenham Bridge on Boundary Road.

98

98 July 1900 Rev. J.M. Bacon & Admiral Sir E. Freemantle D.W. Liddiard

Rev. Bacon met the Admiral on board the Allen liner "Parisian" en route to Liverpool from Montreal. The Admiral showed interest in a balloon flight, the upshot being rather more of an adventure than the Admiral envisaged. There were four of them in the basket, one being Bacon's son, and their flight path took them into the midst of a thunder and hail storm. Eventually, the party landed safely in a clearing in Savernake Forest.

Rev. John Mackenzie Bacon, born in 1846, was an extraordinary man. He moved to Cold Ash in 1876 and lived there until his death in 1904. One of the foremost pioneer balloonists of his era, he also created the Cold Ash hand-bellringers and for a few years was clerical assistant to his friend Hon. Rev. J.H. Nelson at Shaw Church. It is therefore fitting that Newbury District Museum are now housing the British Balloon Museum and Library collections.

99

99 c1910 May Day at Donnington Castle

Nothing is known about the children depicted here or the precise date, it is included as an example of a small local photographer's work of a traditional English custom. F.H. Rolfe lived at 6 York Road and photographed many events in Newbury and district until around 1930.

100 c1907 Newbury Racecourse and Paddock D. Cannings

Newbury Racecourse was the inspired dream of John Porter, a trainer at Kingsclere. The Stewards of the Jockey Club refused Porter a licence to build his racecourse, however on leaving he met King Edward VII on the Club steps and woefully recounted his misfortune.

100

101

The King saw Porter together with his plans the following morning — a licence was duly given. The GWR built a station alongside and ran special trains from Paddington for 10/- first-class return. The inaugural meeting was held on September 26 1905 and was attended by 15,000 spectators.

101 April 1 1933 King George V & Queen Mary
Newbury Racecourse plc

Members of the Royal family have been frequent visitors to Newbury Racecourse since it opened in 1905. King George V is seen here in the unsaddling enclosure shaking hands with (probably) his trainer Jarvis after His Majesty had just seen his own home-bred 4-year-old "Limelight" win the Spring Cup by a short head, ridden by Joe Childs. Gordon (later Sir) Richards was third on Fonab. Queen Mary is on the right, and between the King and Queen stands Mr. L.H. Baxendale of Greenham Lodge, with a carnation in his buttonhole, the original owner of the land on which Newbury Racecourse was built.

102

102 c1890 St. John's Church Mrs. D. Walker
St. John's Church, designed by Butterfield and consecrated in 1860, seen here from St. John's Road. In the background is the Bull (& Dog) Inn, owned by Hawkins of West Mills Brewery, who amalgamated with Atlas Brewery to form the South Berks Brewery in 1898; the Bull and Dog becoming the Church Army Lodging House. The London Apprentice Inn, in the middle of the Newtown Road which many may remember, is obscured by the Church. It was demolished in 1951. In February 1943 most of the church was destroyed by a direct hit from a lone German bomber. The present Wellington Arms is on the left of the photograph.

103

104

105

103 c 1865 Newtown Road looking north
Newbury Library, now in Newbury District Museum
Another early photograph, showing St. John's Church opposite the Lancastrian Boys school, hidden by the villas. Those up to the nearest one [No.52] were destroyed by enemy action in 1943. Church & Child's almhouses, built in 1879, are to the south of No.52, although not then built. On the left is open ground [Thorn & Sons/ St. John's school] to the north of Newtown Cemetery which was opened in 1847. The large building beyond is the old London Apprentice Inn — it was in the middle of the road and traffic could pass either side. The row of five cottages behind have been recently renovated by the Council: they were then called Hereford Place. The building on the far left of the picture is probably the old Bull and Dog; the white cottages were demolished within living memory. A large tree masks The Litten and beyond to the right is No.72 Bartholomew Street, still standing but in a bad state of repair.

104 May 1935 Camp Close Mrs. E. Thorn
One of a pair of photographs taken at the Camp Close Silver Jubilee tea party, the children using their new Jubilee mugs. Many of the people can be named — Olive, Nancy, Lilian, Chris & Edna Pearce, Lillian Patridge, Christine Frost, Katherine and Ray Heap, Bill Rumbold, Kenny Brunsden, June Wellond, Peggy Rush, Mrs. Peal and Archibald, Mrs. Turner, Fred Smith, Bobby Goff, Freda Longmate, Mr. & Mrs. Woodley and children, Mrs. Bowers, Ken, Gavin & Kath Clayton, Ronnie Shepherd, Mrs. Simmons, Elsie Gore & Mr. Piper.
[Sandleford Rise]

105 c1890 Falkland Memorial, Wash Common
Berkshire Archeological Society
Wash Common was enclosed in 1858, later than some other local areas. The first Battle of Newbury (September 1643) was fought around the Wash Common and Enborne Heath area. Lucius Cary, Viscount Falkland, who had been Charles I's Secretary of State, was killed in a cavalry charge near Wash Farm, and in September 1878 a memorial was unveiled by the Earl of Carnarvon to commemorate the 6,000 officers and men who had been killed in the battle 235 years before.
The photograph is taken to the south-west, Andover Road is in the foreground and Battledene Estate lies behind the iron fence. On the right are the houses along Essex Street. The photograph is so sharp, one almost expects the sheep to walk off the page, although guarded by a watchful sheep dog on the right.

106

106 1898 The Gun Public House D. Stubbs
A photograph from the sale catalogue of The Gun and the London Apprentice (Newtown Road) in 1898, both owned by Hawkins Brewery. An inn has been known on the site from the mid-1600's. The building depicted is not much altered today, but the inn sign has changed over the years to represent more up to date armoury.
The Wash Common area was developed after the turn of the century as a separate village and by 1920 had 300 inhabitants. At that time wireless aerials were beginning to sprout in back gardens, and in 1926 a local resident complained bitterly the street lighting was so bad he couldn't see his way to the local Post Office!

107 1905 Form IV, Newbury Girls School
Possibly taken in the area behind the Technical Institute in Northbrook Street [Brook House]. The school opened there the previous year with Esther Luker as headmistress of 38 pupils divided into four forms. Miss Ludwig was her assistant and quite a few well known Newbury families appear on this photograph.

Back row, left-right. D. Rosier. D. Hollands. B. Watts. P. Sharpes. E. Hudson. M. Adnams. A. Edmonds. D. Kimber. H. Freemantle. A. Bunting.
Middle row. E. Smith. E. Bell. W. Hawke. Miss Ludwig. G. Brooks. D. Lake. A. Bishop.
Front row. G. Salway. B. Boyd. K. Plenty. E. Southam. A. Bowditch.

107

108

108 c1930 Girls High School

109 Esther Luker 1904-1934

St. Bartholomew's

The school, now of 100 pupils, moved from Northbrook Street to Andover Road in 1910. By 1914 it had 250 pupils. Esther Luker, a radical headmistress with educational horizons far in advance of her fellows, instituted a school council in 1920 and strongly believed in the equity of higher education for girls. She retired in 1934 and died in 1969 at the age of 97.

An unusual view of the back of the school showing the tennis courts, the pupils in regulation black slips and stockings, the senior pupils in black skirts and white blouses.

The attractive c1784 terrace of stucco houses 61, 63, 65 (&67) Andover Road can be seen in the left background.

109

110

110 c1922 Newbury Grammar School, from Fifth Road

111 E. Sharwood-Smith MA 1903-24

St. Bartholomew's

A chantry school was founded by a bequest of Henry Wormestall in 1466. During the 1800's the school was at the Litten, Newtown Road. The present buildings, designed by Mr. Power of London, were opened in 1885.

Edward Sharwood-Smith became headmaster in 1903 with 40 pupils, but by 1922 he had built up the school's reputation to such an extent that there were 250 pupils. He chose the school's motto *Ad Lucem*, and during his headship he continually campaigned for better facilities; consequently four additional buildings were erected. In 1972 the school was honoured by a visit of Her Majesty the Queen who toured the school and grounds and unveiled a stained glass window to commemorate the school's Quincentenary in 1966.

In 1975 the Girls High and Boys Grammar became St. Bartholomew's Comprehensive, the two areas of buildings perpetuating the names of Wormestall and Luker.

111

112 c1916 Newbury Hospital S. Thomas

A hospital was started in Enborne Terrace in c1880 as an outcome of the injuries caused to the navvies working on the Didcot/Newbury/Southampton railway line. A 12 bed hospital was built on its present site in 1885, extensions being added over the years, with wards named after local benefactors. During World War I, the hospital nursed back to health the wounded from France, as seen here on the lawn fronting the Andover Road.

113 c1904 Raymonds Cottages, Argyle Road

They are situated in "The City", an ancient part of the town where for many years the custom of having their own Mayor of Bartlemas was celebrated — an excuse for a good meal and a

112

113

night out at the Bull & Dog from all accounts. The almhouses, established by Philip Jemmett in 1676, had fallen into disrepair by 1929. Dr. Essex Wynter purchased them together with Bartholomew Manor and philanthropically restored them all, unfortunately altering them out of all recognition using bricks and timber from the area. The Brewer's Company carved arms were re-incorporated into the building on a long pitched gable with pendant. What stands there today is very different from this photograph — the chimney stacks giving a guide-line to what was originally where.

114

115

114 c1915 Kimber's Corner

115 1932 Miss E. Kimber

Newbury District Museum

"Kimber's Corner" was for many years a leading grocer in the town — their horse-drawn delivery vehicle stands outside. The windows are packed with groceries and Gilbey's spirits. Miss Elsie Kimber was Newbury's first lady Mayor in 1932; she retired from the business in 1953 after 64 years connection with the family shop. In Newbury District Museum is the well-known lithograph of the "Making of the Newbury Coat" in 1811; the little girl standing on the right under the tree with a claret-coloured dress and white pinny is said to be an ancestor of Elsie Kimber.

116 1908 Newbury Station from Blackboys Bridge

S. Thomas

The Great Western Railway, designed by Isambard Kingdom Brunel, ran west from Paddington Terminus in London. The photograph shows the station prior to the layout being widened to twice its original width to enable through-lines to be used by west country express trains. Newbury Station had become a busier junction than was envisaged when the station was constructed in the mid-1840's because of the Lambourn Valley and the Didcot/Newbury/Southampton lines passing through the town.

116

117

The coaches on the left are typical c1890 clerestory stock in pre-1908 chocolate and cream livery. The Newbery's Furniture van at the rear is a privately owned "lift van" used for furniture removals, lifted onto the carter's van by crane in the Goods Yards — the lifting point can be seen on the van's roof. A water tank and railway sheds are behind; the Railway Hotel can be seen in the far right background.

117 c1907 Bartholomew Street D. Collins
One of only two located photographs of the southern end of Bartholomew Street. There is an alley alongside a private house, where St. Michael's Road is now, the view immediately recognisable to-day. The turning to Craven Road is clearly visible, and those not clustered round Brindley the fishmonger at No.88 are pursuing their leisurely way so slowly across the street that only one foot has blurred during the time necessary to take the photograph. A horse and cart ambles along in the middle of the road towards St John's.

118

119

118 c1906 The Eight Bells to Blackboys Bridge
The Eight Bells dates from the 16th century, and was restored to its former condition by George Suggett in 1970. An old gentleman stands in the entrance to Trafalgar Place where there were 13 houses, long since gone. Lewis the pork butcher is in his doorway. Swaite's boot & shoe warehouse can be seen clearly advertised on the right, next to Mr. Taylor (see next plate). The entrance to the 1841 Phoenix Brewery (recently restored to its former dignity as their offices by Lyons, Sleeman & Hoare, architects) and Phoenix House, lately Council Offices, followed by a rather sombre-fronted trio of houses, carry on up the well-nigh deserted west side to Blackboys hotel the other side of the railway bridge.

119 c1909 49 Bartholomew Street J. Taylor
Albert Taylor, photographed here with his lather boy, moved from No.46 c1907 and traded at No.49 as a Gunsmith as well as running a men's hairdressing business until 1947. The Taylor family lived over the shop, like most shopkeepers of the era. Living next door to the Phoenix Brewery however, had its hazards, as the bees and wasps imbibed too well at the sticky residue left on the brewing pipes and fell to earth stone drunk in the Taylor's back garden, stinging the children on many occasions.

[Giddy & Giddy, Thake & Paginton]

120

120 November 1894 Craven Street P. Hassell
It had been raining for three weeks and by mid-November West Mills, Kennet Road, Craven Road and Street were flooded. Everyone living in Craven Street retreated to their bedrooms and some can be seen looking out of their windows. A drainage contractor's cart has been wrecked in mid-street. The road was barricaded as water had entered the gas pipes. Milkmen and newsagents used punts to deliver to the marooned, the man seen here appears to be using a door as a punt. Righton advertised in the "NWN" that photographs of the floods were available at 1/3d and 2/3d each, of which this is one example. [Craven Road]

121

121 c1910 109 Bartholomew Street S. Thomas
Mr. & Mrs. Parr's, fruit and confectionery shop; Mr. Parr was also a wheelwright. The left hand window shows plates of different fruits, probably in the Autumn, as one plateful looks like plums; jars of sweets are arranged "soldier" fashion in the other. The Parrs were also parcel receiving agents for the Great Western Railway. Above the shop at first-floor level is a rough iron rod, possibly for hanging meat, although the previous occupant was an upholsterer. It is an almost domestic scene, long since vanished. [Fosters/Field & Stream]

122

122 c1890 Bartholomew Street Sansome & George
This almost static scene was probably taken on a Sunday afternoon from outside Inch's old shop [Tile and Wall Finds/Trencherwood] with its hanging gas lamp. The turning to Market Street is just before Herborough House where Dr. Richard Hickman, who prevented a major smallpox epidemic in 1903, lived. The Primitive Methodist church house is on the left; the next two shops are firmly shut. Dr. Hemstead's elegant 18th century house [Charles, Lucas & Marshall] stands unaltered to-day opposite the present Bus Station. The remainder is a view of long ago.

123 February 26 1929 Market Street R.L. Gibbs
The funeral procession of Mr. William Brain, the founder of W. Brain & Son Ltd. coal merchants. He died on the 22nd from pneumonia, and many other elderly people also died that month from the extremely cold weather. In his young days William Brain was appointed Station Master at Lambourn and virtually ran the Lambourn Valley Railway until he founded a coal business in Lambourn, later moving to Newbury around the time of World War I. His coffin was conveyed to Newtown Cemetery on the firm's black draped trolley, drawn by immaculately groomed black carthorses. The second trolley was purple draped and carried the remainder of the floral tributes; it was followed by the family mourners in the closed carriages. Many people still remember the huge lump of coal displayed in the Market Street office window.

123

124

124 December 1924 Cattle Market
Dreweatt, Watson & Barton
Although this was the centre of the surrounding farming area, it has been rarely photographed. Mr. Arthur T. Watson, with gavel raised, was a partner of Dreweatt, Watson & Barton (founded in 1759) and is selling pigs in the Market just before Christmas. The variety of headgear in this nearly all-male preserve ranges from flat hats to curly-brimmed bowlers — Mr. Watson sporting an enormous droopy brimmed hat which he always wore.
Fatstock markets were held at the Three Tuns Inn [Queens Hotel] in the 1800's and various inns in the town, then later behind Cheap Street. The "new" Cattle Market was opened in 1873 and closed in 1968. [Multi-storey carpark]

125

125 July 19 1911 Diocesan Missions Festival
Newbury District Museum

An all day assembly of the Diocese of Oxford Annual Missionary Festival was held in Newbury in 1911, the afternoon meeting being held at Goldwell Park, Speen Hill, by the kindness of Rev. O. Slocock's widow. At 11.30am the clergy processed from St. John's Church to a Thanskgiving Service in the Parish Church. The St. Nicolas' banner is followed by the clergy of Newbury diocese, then the Pastoral cross bearer near a waiting horse and trap, and finally the Bishop of Oxford and Archdeacons of Berkshire, Bucks, and Oxfordshire. The procession is seen here in Bartholomew Street passing the Tiger Inn and Higgs the pork butcher. In medieval times both sites were used as a hostel by students travelling between William of Wykeham's two colleges, one at Winchester and the other New College Oxford. Davis the hairdresser is next door to New Brothers, mealmen, with their large entrance wide open.

126

126 c1907 Bartholomew Street
A leisurely view of mid-Bartholomew Street. A couple of Gordon Boys stand outside College House, Miss Pollard's school for girls, with the Falkland Arms next door. Whitehorns handcart, advertising Hovis bread with delivery baskets atop, waits before the Church Army Lodging House, marked with a cross by its young postcard sender. On the left is a horse and cart outside Davis, the hairdresser, Higgs the pork butcher and salt merchant is beyond, then the Tiger Inn of somewhat dubious repute, and G.E. Whitehorns the baker with another of his delivery carts outside, horsedrawn for the more outlying rounds. Most of the depicted buildings were either demolished during 1971 in Ravenseft Phase I, or have been altered out of all recognition.

127

127 c1885 16-20 Bartholomew Street R.L. Gibbs
A photograph full of character, with Edwell at No.20, ironmongers, with a large kerbside display of shovels, spades and forks alongside a tricycle.
Mr. Edwell is possibly the man near the gas street lamp, the metal hanging kettle reflected on the brickwork. At No. 19 are Freebody & Dibley, butchers, established in 1864; notice the cellar under the window [Newbury Building Society]. Orams the watchmaker has a wooden barrow outside. The large open door is the entrance and house to Atlas Brewery, which amalgamated with Hawkins in 1898 to become South Berks Brewery on the Bartholomew Street site, when the fascia of No.19 was presumably altered.
[vacant office/Buckell & Ballard]

128

128 1935 Directors & Executive Staff, Newbury Building Society Newbury Building Society
It was registered as the Newbury Permanent Benefit Building Society on November 12 1856 at 62 Northbrook Street. The first Directors were Frederick Talbot the promoter, Messrs. J. Blacket, F. Davis, C.W. Doe, E. Hanington, J.P. Jackson, W.C. Lay, J.H. Lucas, H. Hawe Mason, E. Seymour, J. Staples, and E. & W. Wilson.
It was incorporated in 1893, concurrently taking over the ailing Newbury Industrial Building Society.
The photograph shows the Directors and senior staff at the time the Society moved to its present site at 17-19 Bartholomew Street. A couple of points of interest — John Green (top left) has recently retired after 49 years with the NBS and Harold Bance (front row, far left) refused to sit in a straight line with the other Directors, and moved his chair slightly askew!
Top row, left to right: J.W. Green, W.T. Tobias, G.G. Stevens.
Middle row: F.R. Bance 1932. G.P. Hopson 1931. S.G. Povey, Secretary. J.T. Louch, Solicitor, A.G. Herbert 1931. Cllr. W.H. Bentley 1933. J.D. Robinson 1935.
Front row: E.H. Bance 1926. Cllr. L.E. Shergold FAI 1921. Ald. E. Parfitt JP, CC 1894. Ald. J. Stradling JP 1908, Chairman. J. Johnson 1878. Cllr. C.W. Burns 1911. P. Chillingworth 1918.

129

129 c1920 16 Bartholomew Street S. Hall
Newbury appears to have been well catered for in boot repairs, the town then had a dozen shops selling shoes. A large establishment, Mr. River's employed four other men, assuming he is standing in the doorway. The business started on these premises around World I and closed during the 1950's. The right hand window

displays advertisements for various boot repair products above tins of polish on cards, with some already sold. Rt. Legg painted the shop sign above the door, he inscribed his name under "RY" of Factory. The hanging posters leave nothing to the imagination, but in those days one did not have to quantify one's statements! [Buckell & Ballard]

130 c1905 15 Bartholomew Street
Mrs. F.W. Sampson
Bendy's Bazaar at Christmas time, here advertising, as well as cards, a Dolly Dressing Competition. The windows are laden with tempting toys — the Indian Camp on the bottom shelf was priced at 6/6d. A rocking horse can be seen in the doorway by the card advertising Ladies Umbrellas at 1/11d. The doll's pram hung up in the doorway was available at the special price of 8/9d. [Pearl House]

130

131 c1906 Guildhall Club
A view which has now disappeared. On the left of the Town Hall Clock, the double gables of the Globe Inn can be seen. All the buildings south have been demolished, save one. The Guildhall Club started in Mansion House Street in 1886 and moved to these gothic premises in 1890, a building erected c1850. The club members enjoyed a good library before the Public Library was built, organised many sporting events, patronised photography, and prided itself on being non-political. The balloonist Rev. Bacon and his friend the illusionist Maskelyne were amongst its members. Next door, with the blinds down, is Mr. Willis the bootmaker and then A.C. Bishop cycle works. The low building of the then Bricklayers Arms (still standing) is adjacent to the entrance through Half-moon yard to Cheap Street by the Catherine Wheel. R. Long, ironmonger, can be seen and Harvey the confectioner where the Volunteer's Armoury was kept and Colour-Sergeant Trinder lived.

131

132

132 c1906 "Devon House" 143 Bartholomew Street
A magnificent display photographed at W.F. Porter's, which, judging from the poultry on the ledges, may have been taken at Christmas. The delivery boy has his basket over his shoulder. This building (previously the Co-op.) was demolished recently. Many butchers had their own abattoir behind the premises. Liddiards at 1 Northbrook Street had theirs in Northcroft Lane. The slaughtering commenced behind closed gates at 5.00am and the premises had to be hosed and swept clean before the shops opened. Coldicutts at 85 Northbrook Street had their abattoir at the rear of their shop, but no access to it, so customers were asked to wait in the street while a trained pet sheep led in the animals for slaughter.

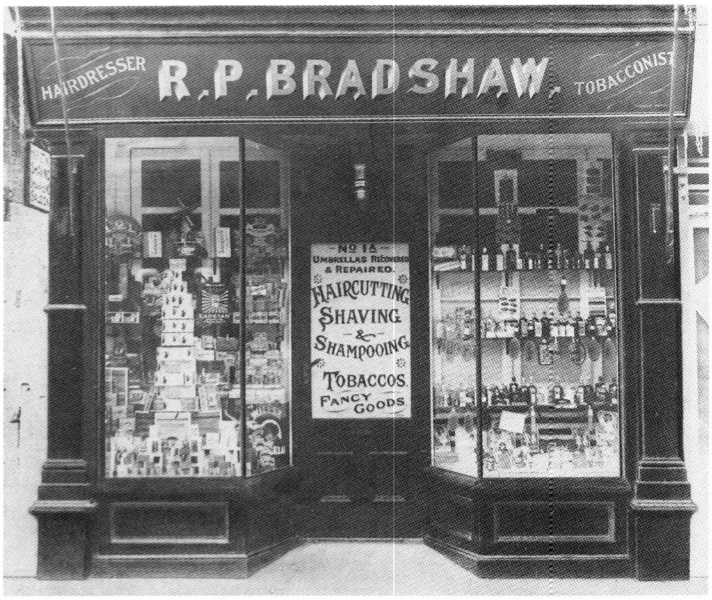

133

133 c1922 No.1a Bartholomew Street
Newbury District Museum
The building was previously owned by Church & Booth, corn dealers and mealmen of Town Mills. No.1, just visible on the right, was used as a dwelling house by the occupiers. Bradshaw's was not only a hairdresser and tobacconist, but an umbrella repairer as well. The windows show a fascinating assortment of goods, in the left hand window, smoker's requirements, cigarettes and matches, on the right hand side shaving brushes, hairbrushes, hand mirrors and (bottom right) an advertisement showing a shingle hairstyle which dates the photograph.

134 c1912 The Arcade
Previously known as Church Lane or Croft. In the Middle Ages it was called Whirleygog Lane, why is not known. Jacksons the clothiers, Benns the confectioners, and Gibsons the jewellers are seen on the left hand side. Jimmy Tufnail's Billiard rooms, tobacconists, hairdressing &

shaving salon are well advertised on the right — it may even be Jimmy himself outside his premises, but as the Arcade was so rarely photographed due to difficulty in obtaining enough light, the man is unclear.

135 c1903 Bartholomew Street looking south

Mrs. F.W. Sampson

Pratts, the old established chemist and druggist, next to the Mansion House. They also supplied animal medicines and a notice in the right hand window states "LOST — one gold watch chain". They display advertisements for "Daisy" to cure "splitting headaches", "One night Corn Cure", and their own brand "Anti-neuralgic Tonic Pills". A large gas lamp with a decorative ironwork fascia and a pair of scrolled supports for window boxes hangs outside the first floor windows. Next door is a small entrance to the caretaker's flat in the Mansion House, then Langfords the drapers, the white panelled gas lights advertising they sold corsets, dresses, hosiery, gloves, millinery and mantles. Burns the jeweller follows; it is still there although the fascia has altered. The Globe Inn can be seen after Jimmy Tufnail's newsagents with four hanging gas lamps, above a large LIBRARY sign advertising Tufnail's circulating library. On the right are the gothic style Portland stone gateways to the Parish Church, erected c1770, with Church & Booth at No.1 just beyond [Bradshaws].

134

135

136

136 July 10 1924 St. Nicolas Parish Church from the air
Part of an aerial photograph from a set of 4 by Aerofilms Ltd and issued as a postcard. St. Nicolas was built on the site of an earlier Norman Church and was completed by 1532. It contains an original Jacobean pulpit, unusual as many church items were desecrated during the time of Cromwell. The four pinnacles and battlements were added during extensive external restoration in 1867. Lloyds Bank, previously London & Counties Bank built in 1867 on the site of the old Globe Inn, stands out clearly, its roof a favourite perch of 20th century pigeons. In Northcroft Lane, east from the Drummer Inn, can be seen the Salvation Army and Temperance Halls and John Childe's Almshouse, virtually the same to-day. In the left foreground are the long buildings at 11a Bartholomew Street of Westcombe's Brewery, bounded on its north side by the Parish Church graveyard. It was closed in 1900 and none of the buildings now remain. The large chestnut tree behind Liddiards at No.1 Northbrook Street [Town Bookseller] had disappeared before 1940.

137

137 c1865 St. Nicolas Church chancel
This photograph of the chancel before extensive internal alterations in 1865, was found in 1912 by the new verger Mr. W.G. Stillman on a local Thursday market stall. A bystander, Mr. Mills a carpenter of West Mill, informed the verger what the photograph depicted. It was eventually given to Mr. J.W.H. Kemp FSA, for 48 years local secretary of the Stained Glass Window Society. He distributed 9 copies — the Bishop of Reading, the Rector, curate and verger and one for the Vestry, Messrs. H. Davis, H.C. Count (churchwardens), W. Edmonds, H.J. Cooke and kept two and the original.

138 A comparative photograph of the chancel in 1910, showing the 1907 Gardiner memorial reredos and how light and airy the chancel became after the alterations. Both photographs were stuck into a copy of Gray's 1839 *History and Antiquities of Newbury*, previously owned by Mr. Kemp. The c1865 photograph had been briefly annotated in shorthand, and the finder Mr. Stillman passed his Pitman's shorthand exam in April 1912!

138

139

139 c1922 St. Nicolas Church choir S. Pocock
Most of the members of the Parish Church choir are pictured here outside the west door. Mr. Sawyer, second row far left, was the organ blower. On occasions he was known to nod off and a small boy was quickly despatched to wake him up and help him blow!
Top row, left-right. Ursell. Unknown. Witts. Unknown.
Second row. Sawyer. Hook. Gregory. Alder. Court. Stillman, verger.
Third row. Hunt. Collins. Plumb. Mitchell. Wilkes. Scott. Stillman. Collins. Pocock.
Fourth row. Andrews. Cox. Barrett. Kingham. Counter. Newman. Cooper. Tilley.
Front row. Collins, (father of the two boys). Hill. Rev. Clayton. Rev. L. Majendie. Bernard Ramsey (organist). Pemberton. Smith. Ferris.

140 c1906 New Town Mill and Miller's House
The building was erected in 1892 after the old Town mill had burnt down in March. It was owned by Church and Booth until acquired by Hovis Ltd. in 1921, then by Doltons in 1956. It was demolished in 1972 and after much controversy flats were erected on the site in 1981.
Church & Booth also had a retail outlet at 1 Bartholomew Street for the sale of animal feed to the public. The left part of the new mill was where the meal was manufactured, and sacks can be seen being loaded into a waggon, under the grain hoist opening. The miller's mid-Georgian town house runs at right angles overlooking the river. The low building on the right was probably the stables and coach house. A pony and light utility trap look to be leaving with a small load for local delivery.
[Town Mill flats]

141 c1916 The Chantry G.T. Osborne
It stands next door to St. Nicholas House in West Mills, built in the 18th century and stuccoed later. It is said the Doric porch originated from the White Hart Hotel in the Market Place. From a photograph of c1871 of the Market Place in the Museum there is no porch at the White Hart Hotel, so perhaps one can presume the porch was in place by c1871.
The photograph depicts four pupils from Miss Pollard's "College House" School for girls, previously in Bartholomew Street, but moving to the Chantry around World War I and remaining there for about six years. The brick built building in the background is now sadly in a state of neglect and decay.

140

141

142

143

142 c1865 West Mills Wharf M. Tanner
An early photographic view of West Mills and its wharf before external additions to the Parish Church in 1867. Another photograph taken at almost the same time is in the Newbury Museum. The South Berks Brewery chimney can be seen in the mid-background, with the Chantry white stuccoed, then enclosed behind a brick wall. Craven House [Brading Barber] with the dormer windows, was sympathetically restored in the early 1970's. Slater's warehouse is at the end next to Thomas Hunt's Almshouses with a round inscribed stone between the windows which is still there to-day. The narrow barge moored alongside the wharf with smoke from the cabin stove, is probably carrying coal from the Somerset coalfields. A horse and cart are backed up alongside the barge ready to load or unload. This is a view that has not radically altered in 120 years, saving the development of flats on the Town Mill site.

143 March 1923 Behind 14 West Mills Mrs. L. Bauer
Leslie (Lil), Tom junior, and Harry Randall, cattle dealers of 10 West Mills; sons of Tom Randall (see Plate 75). By 1925 the Randalls also owned and operated the London Road abattoir [previously Gowrings service repair yard], until meat rationing was introduced during World War II when the Government took over all meat distribution.
The depicted building is virtually unchanged, and in the yard are the remains of the South Berks Brewery stables building.
[Boultons Yard]

144

145

144 c1930 "The Vagabond" Mrs. H. Thompson
Born in 1884, Ernest W. Brockway led an adventurous life in Europe after being educated in Germany. He arrived in London in 1902 and married an artist's model in 1912, served in the Royal Garrison Artillery in World War I, and settled in Kennet Road, Newbury with his wife in the 1920's. He had a bric-a-brac shop there and later rented part of Speenhamland Theatre for storage. He stood 6'6" tall and was often seen pushing his home-made barrow around the town. He died at the local Hospital in 1946. In the 1930's a book was written by him, "ghosted" by F.S. Stuart.

145 1913 Weavers Cottages
These Jacobean cottages formed in all a continuous row westwards of seven. The east gable, shown here, is tile hung with an oriel window and leaded lights, and on the corner is a street light. Below the north gable can be seen a mooring stump for barges with a white-painted upper portion. A painted post and rail of part of the swing bridge to West Mill is in the foreground.
The cottages were modernised and converted into two houses by A.J. Campbell-Cooper in 1963 after purchase by the Council in 1955.
It is not known if these cottages ever did actually house weavers, their previous name was "Vine Cottages".

146

147

148

146 c1910 Barge outing G. Collier
A Sunday outing in one of H. Dolton's canal wide boats, photographed from the towpath near Smallbones Yard. Boat parties to Hamstead Marshall from West Mills were an enjoyable feature of pre-World War I days; canal boat trips are now running again from Newbury Wharf to Hamstead.

147 1892 West Mill looking east
Berkshire Archeological Society
By at least 1500 West Mill was a fulling mill for the finishing of local cloth. Previously it was a corn mill and after the decline of the woollen trade a paper mill, afterwards reverting to corn grinding. It was acquired by Hovis Ltd. in 1921 and re-built, but was almost totally destroyed by fire in 1965 and the area is now under re-development for town houses.
The interesting feature of this very sharp Henry Taunt photograph is the scaffolding round the new town Mill which was completely gutted on March 30 1892 — the west wall of the new Mill is incomplete and crawling boards can be seen on the roof. The new Mill had risen "phoenix-like from the ashes" by December 1892.

148 c1890 Canal bend and old Town Mill
Newbury Weekly News
A tranquil view of the canal with a variety of waterside rooftops reflected in the still water. The delightful bay windows of the miller's house at Town Mills can be seen to the left of the Town Hall clock, and in front is a wall of the lockside garden. Newbury Bridge can just be seen with its white globe shaped light, to the left W.H. Smith's recently vacated premises. The white painted and timber building, together with the adjoining tile-hung building, were recently demolished and both are to be replaced by a "riverside restaurant".

149

149 c1889 Newbury Bridge looking east
The triple-arched bridge was built by James Clarke in 1769, apparently taking three more years to finish at a cost of £700; the two outer arches are incorporated under the adjoining shops. The previous wooden bridge collapsed during a flood in 1726, after which a patched up bridge was utilised. A Hovis lorry drove into the east side of the Bridge in 1928 and seven of the iron balusters ended up in the river. The pair of globe lights were replaced by street ones in 1904, and these were removed after World War II. Note the pair of mooring posts in the foreground for overnight barge mooring. The riverside wooden-faced building of H.C. Count the hatter, and his greenhouse were still there until the early 1930's. Hawkins the bookseller's washing is much in evidence behind four local fishermen complete with bowlers and old fashioned (to us) perch rods.

150

150 1892 Newbury Town Lock
Berkshire Archeological Society
A slightly blurred plate from the lens of Henry Taunt, taken from Newbury Bridge, showing on the left the old footbridge that led to where the Globe Inn stood until 1867. The ducking stool for scolding wives is said to have been at the rear of the Globe [Lloyds Bank plc]. The building with the skylights by the waiting barge horse was used by Hemmins Printing works at the turn of the century. The adjoining cottage was built at the same time as the lock to house the lock keeper, and is now preserved under the care of the British Waterways Board. A full size barge can be seen in the lock waiting for it to be emptied. The continuous rail on the edge of the towpath was most important to allow the horse-lines to run smoothly when the barge was being towed. The barge crew appear to have almost abandoned ship to be photographed.

151

151 1929 Crimea Gun in Victoria Park

Newbury District Museum

The Crimea Gun, one of many given to British towns after 1856, was cast at the Alexandroffsky works in Russia, a 24 pounder weighing 38cwt. Seen here in Victoria Park after its removal from the Broadway, it was placed alongside a World War I German artillery field gun from the Cattle Market, in the area of the present Bandstand. The Russian gun had an extremely chequered career in Newbury — although never locally fired in anger it caused a deal of disturbance. On its arrival by train in the late 1850's, the burghers were at first loathe to pay for its carriage, but eventually the dues were discharged and the gun was placed in the Marsh [Victoria Park]. In 1863 it fired a salute for the Prince of Wales's Wedding and broke many windows in the surrounding houses. It remained there until the Fenian scare in 1868 when some worthy realised the muzzle was pointing at St. Nicolas Church tower. The Fire Brigade removed it forthwith to the Wharf Fire Station. For a time it was mounted on the green near the railway station, taken to the Marsh in 1887 to fire a Jubilee salute and left there lying in the dirt until it was placed in the Broadway by March 1889; removed to the Park again in 1929, and finally both guns were melted down for scrap in the early part of World War II by Plenty's.

152

152 May 16 1910 Victoria Park
The annual Horse Parade was a feature of Whitsun from the turn of the century until World War I. J.H. Digweed's turnout is seen here near the avenue of lime trees in Victoria Park, planted by public subscription in 1883, where the judging took place. There were classes from a pair of carthorses to a light business trap under 14 hands. Mr. Digweed was a butcher of 62 Cheap Street and his very smart chestnut mare came second, winning 10/- in the light business turn-out over 14 hands. The trap was driven by Jack Head.
The area's name was changed from The Marsh to Victoria Park as a tribute to Queen Victoria after her death in 1901.

153

153 c1910 Newbury Wharf
The wharf is so radically altered it is not easy to describe this photograph. The basin was partially filled in during the 1920's, and completely in 1933 to provide a bus station and car parking. From left to right, the dark building is the Granary [Newbury District Museum]; the white gabled Cloth Hall can be seen at a slight angle; then Kendrick House, the Dolton family home with the Town Hall clock (as always) standing guard over the scene. Doltons shed (see plate 50) with its strange double-gable roof is behind the lower long storage shed, in front of which is the lighter coloured Stone building now the headquarters of the Newbury section of the Kennet & Avon Canal Trust. In this photograph the top half of the door is hinged back and alongside is a wooden crane. On the wharf bank are what appear to be low stacks of timber and against the long storage shed sacks of grain. In the right foreground is a horse-bridge on the tow path over the channel leading to a sluice gate, locally called the "mini-hatch" and filled in during 1961.

154

154 c1896 River Kennet & Canal looking east

Berkshire Archeological Society

To end this book, a delightful photograph taken from the tow path showing the horse-gate, just after the point at which the river divides into two. The canal is in the middle and the left hand portion of the river is visible under the overhanging tree. The right hand portion fed round to the light-coloured Greenham Mill, formerly a tanning mill, where the Newbury Coat was made by John Coxeter in 1811. The mill was sold to the Urban Electricity Supply Company in 1903 and converted to supply the town with electricity on December 23 1904 at a cost of 7d a unit. The demolished canalside cottages just beyond are now the site of Pipe Welding Company. In the distance is Greenham footbridge, then a swing bridge, now converted to an overhead one. The cottages beyond were demolished just after the turn of the century to build Hollands Flour Mill, where Alfred Hollands made the first Digestive biscuit to his own recipe of which he was extremely secretive; but he would pay any price asked to obtain the special flour needed.

Sources and Bibliography

Directories:
English 1794
Piggot & Co. 1844
Kelly 1847 and various thereafter
Dutton Allen 1863
Harrods Royal 1876
Cosburn 1883 and various thereafter

History of Newbury — W.H. Money 1887
Popular History of Newbury — W.H. Money 1905
Newbury Scrapbook — V.F.M. Garlick 1970
Newbury Buildings Past & Present — Borough Museum 1973
Newbury District Field Club Transactions 1870-1911, 1930-1983
Newbury 1837-1893 — F.H. Stillman 1893
Local History in England — W.G. Hoskins 1972
Newbury Weekly News 1867-1935 & "Memories Revived" to date

Maps:
Willis 1768
Davis 1849
Ordnance Survey 1880/1 & 1936

For dating photographs:—
Victorian Dress in Photographs — M. Ginsberg 1982
Seasons of Change — S. Ward 1982
A Country Camera 1844-1914 — G. Winter 1973
The Golden Years 1903-1913 — G. Winter 1977
The Birth of Photography — B. Coe 1976

Commercial photographers of plates

Aerofilms Ltd., Borehamwood (Newbury 1924 & 1928)	**136**
L. Blandford, 26 Northbrook Street c1930-50	**38**
E.T. Brooks, 84 Northbrook Street c1860-85	**Frontispiece**
T. Curry, Goswell Place, London Road c1877-1910	**66 75**
P.O. Collier, Reading c1907-40	**26 54 86 116 117 126**
Electric Light Studios, Street & Redstone c1905-08	**13 22 65 107**
H. Harbut, 12 Northcroft Lane c1872-90	**3 5**
Hawker (& Son). West Street, later 84 Northbrook St. c1885-1940	**1 8 12 24 49 70 90 128 153**
J. Hopson, 65 Northbrook St. c1850-60	**56-60**
T.B. Howe, 42 Northbrook Street c1875-93	**127**
E. Longmate, 42 Northbrook Street c1918-1940	**20 53 104**
Parsons of Hungerford c1909-42	**71**
J.W. Righton, 42 Northbrook Street c1885-1918	**48 69 83 120**
F.H. Rolfe, 6 York Road c1900-30	**55 87 99 132 133 143**
Sport & General, London	**101**
H. Taunt, Oxford (in this book c1885-95)	**50 105 147 150 154**
W. Whiley, ?Mansion House Street c1902-10	**113**

Local postcard publishers

C.E. Anderson, Bartholomew Street	**118**
Blacket & Turner, Northbrook Street	**100**
H. Etherton, Cheap Street	**112**
W. Gamble, Northbrook Street	**17 30 46**
A. Green, Cheap Street	**81**
J.E. Pratt, ?Bartholomew Street	**2**

National postcard publishers

M. Carroll & Co., Roehampton	**108**
Judges Ltd., Hastings (Newbury 1913)	**41 145**
Relfe Bros. Ltd., London	**110**
F.G.O. Stuart, Southampton (Newbury 1903)	**91**
J. Valentine, Dundee (Newbury c1905)	**19 27 96**
John Walker & Co., London (Newbury c1903)	**135**
Woolstone Bros., London (Newbury c1908)	**44 131**
Wymans Series (Newbury c1912)	**134**
Wyndhams Series (Newbury c1904)	**42 72**